The Palgrave Lacan Series

Jacques Lacan is one of the most important and influential thinkers of the 20th century. The reach of this influence continues to grow as we settle into the 21st century, the resonance of Lacan's thought arguably only beginning now to be properly felt, both in terms of its application to clinical matters and in its application to a range of human activities and interests. The Palgrave Lacan Series is a book series for the best new writing in the Lacanian field, giving voice to the leading writers of a new generation of Lacanian thought. The series will comprise original monographs and thematic, multi-authored collections. The books in the series will explore aspects of Lacan's theory from new perspectives and with original insights. There will be books focused on particular areas of or issues in clinical work. There will be books focused on applying Lacanian theory to areas and issues beyond the clinic, to matters of society, politics, the arts and culture. Each book, whatever its particular concern, will work to expand our understanding of Lacan's theory and its value in the 21st century.

Robert Samuels

(Mis)Understanding Freud with Lacan, Zizek, and Neuroscience

palgrave
macmillan

Robert Samuels
Writing Program
University of California, Santa Barbara
Goleta, CA, USA

The Palgrave Lacan Series
ISBN 978-3-031-13326-8 ISBN 978-3-031-13327-5 (eBook)
https://doi.org/10.1007/978-3-031-13327-5

Cover illustration: ImageGap / iStock / Getty Images Plus / Getty

This Palgrave Macmillan imprint is published by the registered company Springer Nature Switzerland AG.
The registered company address is: Gewerbestrasse 11, 6330 Cham, Switzerland

Dedicated to Madeleine and Sophia

Contents

1

Introduction

The main argument of this book is that psychoanalytic theory and practice is structured by five threshold concepts, yet these principles are rarely understood—even by psychoanalysts themselves. In examining the original meanings of the pleasure principle, the primary processes, the unconscious, transference, and the reality principle, I hope to provide a stable and clear ground for this important discipline. I will also focus on the many ways these core concepts are distorted and repressed. While the psychoanalyst must remain open and unbiased during treatment in order enable the uncensored free association of the patent, this analytic position is determined by a clear understanding of the theory's key concepts.

I will argue that in his early *Project for a Scientific Psychology*, Freud develops a narrative of human development that will continue to shape his work throughout his life.[1] I consider this unpublished text to be the blueprint and key to psychoanalysis because it presents his five central concepts in one complete system. Freud's early work is also important because it aimed to ground psychoanalysis in neurology; however, Freud also introduces a vital challenge to the brain sciences.[2]

R. Samuels, *(Mis)Understanding Freud with Lacan, Zizek, and Neuroscience*, The Palgrave Lacan Series, https://doi.org/10.1007/978-3-031-13327-5_1

Book Outline

Following this introduction, Chap. 2 offers a close reading of Freud's *Project for a Scientific Psychology* in order to define the original meanings of the pleasure principle, the primary processes, transference, repression, and the reality principle. One of the main arguments of this chapter is that Freud's basic theory is often misunderstood because his central concepts are counter-intuitive and threatening to our own egos and views of society and the mind.[3] Moreover, I stress the close relation between psychoanalytic theory and practice as a way of indicating that any misunderstanding of his original principles results in deviations in treatment.

To help elucidate how these basic psychoanalytic concepts have been misunderstood, in Chap. 3, I read closely Mark Solm's *The Hidden Spring: A Journey to the Source of Consciousness.*[4] With this sustained attempt to combine psychoanalysis and neuroscience, we see how Freud's insights are often distorted and repressed by the new brain sciences. Even though Freud did begin his work as a neurologist, I posit that his anticipation of neuroscientific thinking actually goes against the main arguments of contemporary brain scientists. Moreover, throughout this book, I will claim that psychoanalysis provides the most effective and realistic scientific understanding of the human mind.

Chapter 4 examines Lacan's *The Four Concepts of Psychoanalysis.*[5] Although Lacan also looks at transference and the unconscious, his conceptions of the drives and repetition distort some of Freud's central principles. Furthermore, he often confuses the pleasure principle with the primary processes as he replaces the reality principle with the concept of repetition. Most importantly, Lacan conflates the primary processes with the unconscious as he downplays repression and focuses on how the unconscious is structured like a language.

Chapter 5 looks at Mitchell Wilson's *The Analyst's Desire* in order to show how a contemporary psychoanalyst misunderstands Freud's and Lacan's basic insights.[6] In stressing the role played by the analyst's desire, Wilson reveals why so many analysts resist the analytic process itself. What is so instructive about this work is that is demonstrates how psychoanalysis can be repressed within psychoanalysis.

In Chap. 6, I read Slavoj Zizek's *The Sublime Object of ideology* as an effort to repress the content of psychoanalysis.[7] In his desire to combine Marx, Lacan, and Hegel, we shall see how Zizek ends up producing a cynical theory of cynicism as a new form of behaviorism is equated with ideology and contemporary social practices.

Chapter 7 examines the book *Intersectionality and Psychoanalysis* to explore the conflict between identity politics and psychoanalytic practice.[8] My main argument is that psychoanalytic treatment is centered on the neutrality of the analyst and the free association of the patient, and this open discourse is narrowed and limited by a concern for issues concerning race, gender, and class. My point is not to dismiss these vital social influences; instead, I hope to show how any and every social factor can be voiced in the analytic process.

Method

This book focuses on close readings of specific primary texts in order to examine the actual words and ideas of the authors under consideration.[9] I do not provide a survey of the field; instead, I concentrate on clarifying Freud's key insights, and then I look at some of the ways these concepts are being misunderstood by influential theorists and practitioners. Throughout this work, psychoanalysis is seen as a universal discourse that addresses subjective, cultural, and historical differences. As a product of the Enlightenment, Freud's theories apply the scientific method to everyday experiences and thoughts, and this entails taking an unbiased perspective in relation to material evidence.[10] Thus, while Freud is often attacked for being unscientific, I posit that his method is actually more scientific than many other current approaches to human subjectivity.[11]

While my book does focus on Freud's main concepts, the goal is not to say that Freud is always right or even that he fully understands the implications of his own theories. Since it took him a long time to discover free association and analytic neutrality, his practice often lags behind his theory, and yet his central concepts are also shaped by his clinical experience.[12] Moreover, Freud often uses concepts and metaphors borrowed from biology, chemistry, and physics in order to represent symbolic ideas, and so it is necessary to translate many of his representations from the hard sciences back to rhetoric, psychology, and linguistics.[13]

In grounding my understanding of Freud's concepts through a reading of his *Project for a Scientific Psychology*, I hope to show how at the start of his career, Freud often treated psychological processes as biological structures, while he understood neurology from the perspective of linguistics.[14] It is therefore vital to treat his ideas as metaphors that have to be translated from one discipline into another discipline. As we shall see in the following chapters, many people reading Freud today, simply take his biological metaphors literally as they try to base psychoanalysis on the new brain sciences. This attempt to make psychoanalysis more scientific actually ends up having the opposite effect.

Notes

1. Freud, Sigmund. "Project for a scientific psychology (1950 [1895])." *The Standard Edition of the Complete Psychological Works of Sigmund Freud, Volume I (1886-1899): Pre-Psycho-Analytic Publications and Unpublished Drafts*. 1966. 281–391.
2. Miller, Norman S., and Jack L. Katz. "The neurological legacy of psychoanalysis: Freud as a neurologist." *Comprehensive psychiatry* 30.2 (1989): 128–134.
3. Goldberg, Arnold. *Misunderstanding Freud*. Other Press, 2004.
4. Solms, Mark. *The hidden spring: A journey to the source of consciousness*. WW Norton & Company, 2021.
5. Lacan, Jacques, Jacques-Alain Miller, and Alan Sheridan. *The four fundamental concepts of psycho-analysis*. Routledge, 2018.
6. Wilson, Mitchell. *The Analyst's Desire: The Ethical Foundation of Clinical Practice*. Bloomsbury Publishing USA, 2020.
7. Žižek, Slavoj. *The sublime object of ideology*. Verso Books, 2019.
8. Belkin, Max, and Cleonie White, eds. *Intersectionality and relational psychoanalysis: New perspectives on race, gender, and sexuality*. Routledge, 2020.
9. Schur, David. "An introduction to close reading." *Harvard University: Second Version. [Online]* (1998).
10. Stockholder, Kay. "Lacan versus Freud: Subverting the enlightenment." *American Imago* 55.3 (1998): 361–422.

11. Von Eckhardt, Barbara. "Why Freud's research methodology was unscientific." *Psychoanalysis and Contemporary Thought* 5.4 (1982): 549–574.
12. Steiner, John. "The aim of psychoanalysis in theory and in practice." *International Journal of Psycho-Analysis* 77 (1996): 1073–1083.
13. Yovell, Yoram. "From mechanism to metaphor—On Freud's struggle with the biology of the mind." *Journal of the American Academy of Psychoanalysis* 25.3 (1997): 513–524.
14. Stengel, Erwin. "A Re-Evaluation of Freud's Book" On Aphasia". Its Significance for Psycho-Analysis." *International journal of psycho-analysis* 35 (1954): 85–89.

2

Freud's Project

This chapter argues that Freud's early *Project for a Scientific Psychology* presents the blueprint for psychoanalytic theory and practice.[1] By introducing the core concepts of the pleasure principle, the primary processes, transference, the unconscious, and the reality principle, Freud's text lays the foundations for everything else that would follow in this field. In fact, one can judge the interpreters of his work based on their (mis)understanding of these threshold concepts.[2] As we shall see, it is vital to define each principle separately while one also integrates them into a shared structure. From this perspective, much of Freud's later work and the work of other psychoanalysts is a fleshing out of this unpublished text from 1895.

The Pleasure Principle and the Death Drive

For Freud, the fundamental driving force behind the human mind is the pleasure principle, which he paradoxically defines by the goal of avoiding all unpleasure:

R. Samuels, *(Mis)Understanding Freud with Lacan, Zizek, and Neuroscience*, The Palgrave Lacan Series, https://doi.org/10.1007/978-3-031-13327-5_2

> So far, however, we have only given an incomplete description of the content of consciousness. Apart from the series of sensory qualities, it presents another and very different series-the series of sensations of pleasure and unpleasure. And these we must now interpret. Since we have certain knowledge of a trend in psychical life towards *avoiding unpleasure,* we are tempted to identify that trend with the primary trend towards inertia. (373)

Here Freud posits that pleasure is defined by a law of mental inertia—indicating that we are driven to use as little mental energy as possible, and so we seek to return to a lifeless state of inanimation: "What I have in mind is *the principle of neuronic inertia,* which asserts that neurones tend to divest themselves of quantity" (357). This concept of neural divestment will later result in Freud's theory of the death drive, which is the logical conclusion to the pleasure principle.[3] The goal of life is then paradoxically to escape life itself.

Feud adds that the only thing preventing us from the realization of total inertia is the desire caused by internal unmet needs:

> From the very first, however, the principle of inertia is upset by another set of circumstances. As the internal complexity of the organism increases, the neuronic system receives stimuli from the somatic element itself-endogenous stimuli, which call equally for discharge. These have their origin in the cells of the body and give rise to the major needs: hunger, respiration and sexuality. The organism cannot withdraw itself from them as it does from external stimuli. (356)

Competing with the drive to eliminate all stimulation and tension, we find the internal demands of the drives and unmet needs. Since these desires cannot be removed by a reflexive fight or flight reaction, they have to be dealt with in another way.

As a core principle of psychoanalysis, desire is the central force countering the death drive of the pleasure principle: "The neuronic system is consequently obliged to abandon its original trend towards inertia (that is, towards a reduction of its level of tension to zero). It must learn to tolerate a store of quantity sufficient to meet the demands for specific action" (357). The need to have sex, to breathe, and to eat are therefore posited as primary counter-forces, which make possible the storing of energy to perform a specific action in the external world.[4]

In starting with Freud's initial theory of the pleasure principle, we see that most of psychoanalysis can be explained by a single narrative of development. Freud argues in the *Project* that the first way humans are able to satisfy the law of inertia and our internal desires is by hallucinating a scene of satisfaction; when this primary process fails to achieve its goal, the next stage is to cry out for help so that someone else can make the unpleasure go away through a process of transferring responsibility. Eventually, one has to accept the reality of dis-satisfaction, and so the reality principle replaces the pleasure principle. In moving from the pleasure principle to the primary processes to transference to the reality principle, Freud articulates four of the five key concepts. The fifth concept revolves around the fact that people lie to themselves about their own desires and fears, and in this act of repression, the unconscious is born.[5]

It will be my argument throughout this book that if one does not understand these fundamental concepts, one will not be able to think in a psychoanalytic manner. Moreover, it is vital to trace some of the ways these core notions are distorted and misunderstood. In fact, the misunderstanding of psychoanalysis sheds light on the process of repression itself since ultimately what is being avoided is the reality of our own minds.

What Is Consciousness?

Freud's first radical move is to posit that humans have an automatic ability to satisfy the pleasure principle through hallucination: "I have no doubt that the wishful activation will in the first instance produce something similar to a perception-namely, a hallucination" (381). Within the context of the primary processes, the desire to fulfill the pleasure principle results in the confusion between the memory of a similar scene of satisfaction and the perception of the external world.[6] According to this logic, our minds automatically seek to replace unmet needs with the memory of a past event. It is then this confusion that defines for Freud the origins of consciousness and thought itself.

To clarify this connection between thought and hallucination, we can look at perhaps the most famous argument in Western philosophy, which is Descartes' "I think, therefore, I am."[7] What is important to note is that right before he makes this affirmation, he argues that even if he does not know if he is awake or dreaming, what he knows is that in both states, he is thinking. In fact, Descartes posits that we never know for sure if we are dreaming or awake, and so on the level of pure thought and consciousness, there is no distinction between reality and an imaginary fictional world.[8] Moreover, what Descartes does not say is that on the level of dreams, we do not control our own thinking, and so not only are we prone to avoid reality, but we also do not have mastery over our own minds.[9]

For Freud, dreams are clear evidence of the hallucinatory nature of the primary processes and the most basic mode of consciousness: "Ideas in dreams are of a hallucinatory nature; they awaken consciousness and meet with belief. This is the most important characteristic of dreams. It becomes obvious at once in alternate fits of sleeping and waking. One shuts one's eyes and hallucinates, one opens them and thinks in words" (401). From this perspective, whenever we dream, we hallucinate since we confuse internal thoughts with the perception of the external world. In what he will later call the "omnipotence of thought" in animistic culture, Freud stresses that our "primitive" minds function by eliminating the difference between the inner and outer worlds.[10]

While dreams and hallucination may appear to be extreme mental states, Freud insists that the primary processes structure our thoughts and memories: "we might turn back to the nature of the primary process and point out that the primary recollection of a perception is always a hallucination and that it is only inhibition on the part of the ego which has taught us never to cathect… in such a way that it can transfer cathexis retrogressively …" (401). From this radical perspective, our primary way of thinking and recalling memories relies on the primary processes and the hallucinatory repetition of a previous event. In fact, Freud adds that the goal of dreams is the fulfilment of wishes through hallucination:

> The purpose and meaning of dreams (or at least of normal ones) can be established with certainty. Dreams are *the fulfilments of wishes*-that is, pri-

> mary processes following on experiences of satisfaction; and they are not recognized as such, merely because the release of pleasure (the reproduction of pleasurable discharges) in them is slight, since in general they run their course almost without affect *(i.e.,* without motor release). But it is very easy to prove that this is their nature. And it is for this very reason that I am inclined to infer that *primary wishful cathexes too are of a hallucinatory character.* (402)

In arguing that the fundamental way we satisfy the dictates of the pleasure principle is through the hallucination of scenes of satisfaction, Freud offers a new way of thinking about thought and consciousness. It turns out that at the foundation of what makes us different from all other animals is our ability to confuse memories with perceptions.

This fundamental confusion structuring consciousness in the primary processes is also related by Freud to the essence of human emotions: "In a word, the affective process approximates to the uninhibited primary process" (415). The key then to our emotional reactions is that they are determined by the same processes that we find in dreams and hallucinations, which concerns their ability to suspend reality testing through a process of unintentional symbolic associations: "The connections in dreams are partly nonsensical, partly feeble-minded or even meaningless or strangely demented. The last of these attributes is explained by the fact that the compulsion to associate prevails in dreams, as no doubt it does primarily in all psychical life. Two cathexes that are simultaneously present must, so it seems, be brought into connection with each other" (400). This automatic compulsion to associate different representations that occur at the same time provides the foundations for our access to language and symbolic thought.[11] As a fundamental mode of rhetoric, metaphor, and poetry, the connecting of two separate things through their shared temporal presence provides the possibility for creative thought and imagination.[12]

As Lacan will later claim, what defines the essence of symbolic language is that one signifier represents the subject for another signifier, and we find this same logic in Freud's theory of associative thinking.[13] In fact, Freud provides a direct example of this structure: "The knight who fights for a lady's glove *knows,* in the first place, that the glove owes its importance to the lady; and, secondly, his worship of the glove does not in the least prevent him from thinking of the lady and serving her in other ways" (407). The core idea here is that the glove acts as a signifier that is related to the signifier of the lady. Here we find the root of Lacan's claim that the unconscious is structured like a language, but in Freud's example, it is not a question of the unconscious since there is no repression. Instead, Freud is pointing to how consciousness itself is structured like a symbolic language.

This same logic of symbolic association and metaphoric substitution is used by Freud to define neural structures and the very possibility of memory itself: "We can then assert that *memory is represented by the facilitations existing between the neurone" (361).* By positing that memories are constituted through the connection between different neurons, he is treating these memories as if they are signifiers connected in a network of associations. What most contemporary neuroscientists, however, do not accept is this idea that neurons as signifiers have no inherent presence because they are defined in relation to other signifiers; likewise, memories are not stable representations since their meaning is determined by their relation to other memories, and the same structure applies to thought itself.[14]

In an insight that anticipates structural linguistics, Freud affirms that signifiers are defined by their difference to other signifiers: "It is therefore more correct to say that memory is represented by the *differences* in the facilitations between the neurons" (361). Here we see how memories are open to constant revision and distortion because they are not self-contained or permanent, stable representations; as a system of networked differences and associations, the primary processes function through substitution and displacement.[15] Our minds, then, have an automatic poetic essence since our memories are structured through metaphor (substitution) and metonymy (displacement). Freud explains this associative network in the following manner: "Every neuron must in general be presumed to have several paths of connection with other neurones--that is, several contact-barriers. It is on this that the possibility depends of the excitation having a choice of path, determined by facilitation" (363). Here Freud anticipates the foundations of modern linguistics, computer science, and neuroscience since he defines the fundamental processes of differentiation, association, and substitution in a network of connections, but what he adds to these structures is the key mutation of hallucination as the prototype of consciousness.[16] Just as genetic evolution revolves around mutations as coding errors, the confusion between the perception of the external world and internal mental representations (memories) defines the possibility of thought and consciousness.

It is important to stress that in order to decode Freud's *Project,* one has to realize that he is treating biology, psychology, and linguistics through the same set of concepts. In other terms, he does not differentiate between the brain and the mind since he sees neurons as both physical and mental elements. In fact, we shall see that his work anticipates much of contemporary neuroscience and computer science because his structural model equates neural hardware with representational software.[17] However, Freud goes beyond the new brain sciences by defining consciousness through the combination of associative thinking and the confusion between memories and perceptions.

Freud insists that psychoanalysis is the only science that can define consciousness because the other sciences are unable to account for the relation between physical and subjective experiences:

> According to a modern mechanistic theory, consciousness is no more than an appendage added to physiologico-psychical processes, an appendage whose absence would make no difference to the course of psychical events. According to another theory consciousness is the subjective side of all psychical events and is thus inseparable from physiologico-mental processes. The theory which I have here propounded lies between these two. According to it consciousness is the subjective side of a *part* of the physical processes in the neuronic system-namely, of the *perceptual* processes (co-processes). (372)

For Freud, then, only psychoanalysis allows us the ability to link subjective consciousness of the mind to the mechanical structures of the brain. The paradox of this focus on subjectivity is that Freud also states that we have no personal awareness of how our own consciousness works.

In examining the hallucinations of psychotics, primitive belief systems, and dreams, Freud reveals the ways our minds generate a fundamental confusion between reality and imagination in order to avoid unpleasure.

Moreover, since we cannot control these processes, the sense of intentionality is only an illusion created by our egos, which themselves are defined by their ability to radically misrecognized and repress both internal and external reality.[18] Dreams, then, play an important role in analytic practice because they provide proof of the primary processes, which themselves serve to structure the foundation of our mental life. It is not only that hidden truths are displayed in our dreams—what we discover in our recounting of these representations is that we are not in control of our own minds, and our thoughts are fundamentally symbolic and poetic. It is due in part to the automatic nature of the primary process that Lacan says that the subject of the dream is always missing or barred.[19] What we find in psychotic hallucinations and the dream state is the same unintentional tendency to project internal mental representations onto the external world. Freud then uses his understanding of psychosis and dreams to posit that the infant hallucinates the object of desire, and so one of Freud's great leaps of thought is to draw this analogy among dreamers, psychotics, and infants.[20]

Although it would be easy to dismiss hallucinations as extreme states disconnected from our daily lives, Freud's wager is that our ability to imagine a reality that does not actually exist is both the greatest strength and the greatest weakness of humans. On the positive side, we are able to anticipate the future and create alternatives to the current world, but on the negative side, our mental freedom can result in a loss of reality and rationality. Since Freud defines thought itself as experimental action, he shows how humans can not only satisfy their desires and the dictates of the pleasure principle on an imaginary level, but they are also able to project themselves into the future as they re-interpret their past.[21]

Transference and the Demand

Freud posits that when the hallucination of satisfaction fails to quell the desires of unmet needs, the initial reaction of the infant is to cry or scream. We shall see in the following key passage that this "specific action" forms the foundation of social morality and communication for psychoanalysis:

> Experience shows that the first path to be followed is that leading to *internal change* (e.g., emotional expression, screaming, or vascular innervation). But, as we showed at the beginning of the discussion, no discharge of this kind can bring about any relief of tension, because endogenous stimuli continue to be received in spite of it and the tension is re-established. Here a removal of the stimulus can only be effected by an intervention which will temporarily stop the release of quantity in the interior of the body, and an intervention of this kind requires an alteration in the external world (e.g., the supply of nourishment or the proximity of the sexual object), and this, as a "specific action", can only be brought about in particular ways. At early stages the human organism is incapable of achieving this specific action. It is brought about by extraneous help, when the attention of an experienced person has been drawn to the child's condition by a discharge taking place along the path of internal change [e.g., by the child's screaming]. This path of discharge thus acquires an extremely important secondary function--viz., of bringing about an understanding with other people; and the original helplessness of human beings is thus the primal source of all moral motives. (379)

As a core principle of psychoanalysis, when the baby's cry is interpreted as a call for help by caregivers, the fundamental relation between the self and the Other is established.[22] In this transference of responsibility, it is now the Other who must satisfy the unmet need. This theory explains why Lacan insists that the subject's demand to the Other is actually a demand for love, recognition, and understanding.[23] After all, the caregiver has to recognize the crier and understand what the cry means. Moreover, by saying that this specific action is the primal source of our moral motives, Freud posits that our individual helplessness makes us dependent on other people, and this dependency drives social morality and communication.

The true meaning of transference in psychoanalysis thus relates to this fundamental relationship between the helpless subject and the responding Other. As Lacan posits, one reason why the patient may fall in love with the doctor is that the doctor is seen as being able to satisfy the patient's demand for love, knowledge, and recognition.[24] In fact, an analytic treatment begins with this demand, but eventually, this type of transference has to be overcome. Transference is then a necessary obstacle to the task of analysis because analysis starts with a demand for help and ends with the growing independence of the patient, and it is this goal of separation that is often refused by contemporary analysts and therapists.[25]

As we shall see, Freud develops his theory of analytic treatment by moving away from his initial practice of hypnosis.[26] One reason for this change in technique is that Freud found that he could get people to change when they were under hypnosis, but this change would only last a short amount of time, and many people could not be hypnotized at all.[27] Freud also found that the less he interpreted, the more people were able to discover on their own the causes for their psychological issues. By remaining neutral, Freud enabled the process of free association, which in turn allowed the patient to encounter the reality of their own repressed thoughts and feelings.[28] In placing the onus of responsibility back onto the patient, Freud was able to reduce the role played by transference as the patient gained a stronger sense of independence. However, Freud still had to deal with repression and the various other defenses blocking free association, and so he had to develop his theory of the unconscious, which we will see was first produced through his clinical interaction with hysterical patients.[29]

The Unconscious

For Freud, hysterics posed a problem for doctors because their symptoms did not make anatomical or cognitive sense:

> Every observer of hysteria is at once struck by the fact that hysterical patients are subject to a *compulsion,* which is operated by means of *excessively intense ideas.* An idea may emerge into consciousness with special frequency, without the course of events justifying it; or it may be that the arousing of this neurone is accompanied by psychical consequences which are unintelligible. The emergence of the excessively intense idea has results which, on the one hand, cannot be suppressed and, on the other hand, cannot be understood: releases of affect, motor innervations, inhibitions. (405)

In this definition of hysteria, the key aspect of symptoms is the compulsion to think excessively intense ideas that cannot be understood and do not seem to match the manifest cause. While the subject is aware of the strangeness of these thoughts and feelings, they remain incomprehensible for both the patient and the doctor: "They are ideas which produce no effects in other people and whose importance we cannot appreciate. They appear to us as intruders and usurpers and accordingly as ridiculous" (405). While other doctors simply dismissed or demonized these hysterical productions, Freud sought to understand them by seeking out their hidden causes.[30]

By listening to the words of these neglected and dismissed subjects, Freud shows that he is willing to follow the truth where ever it takes him, and what he discovers is that the reactions of these hysterics make sense if one realizes that they are based on an understandable cause that has been hidden through a process of substitution and displacement:

> *Before* the analysis, *A* is an excessively intense idea, which forces its way into consciousness too often, and each time it does so leads to tears. The subject does not know why *A* makes him weep and regards it as absurd--but he cannot prevent it. *After* the analysis, it has been discovered that there is an idea *B* which rightly leads to tears and which rightly recurs often until a certain complicated piece of psychical work directed against it has been completed by the subject. The effect of *B* is not absurd, is comprehensible to the subject and can even be fought against by him. (406)

The key move here is to seek out the reason for unreason by returning to the symbolic network of the primary processes. In treating memories and thoughts as signifiers, Freud is able to trace the movement of symbolic substitution and displacement.[31]

This theory of the formation of neurotic symptoms shows why Lacan insisted that the unconscious is structured like a language since it is clear that Freud is using the main principles of modern structural linguistic before this discipline was developed. In fact, the following passage shows Freud's logical and rhetorical approach to the structure of mental representations and memories: "*B* stands in a particular relation to *A*. For there has been an event which consisted of *B* +*A*. *A* was a subsidiary circumstance, while *B* was well calculated to produce a lasting effect. The production of this event in memory now occurs as though *A* had taken *B's* place. *A* has become a substitute, a "symbol", for B. Hence the incongruity; for *A* is accompanied by consequences which it does not seem to deserve, which are not appropriate to it" (406–407). The hysterical symptom is thus produced through a production of a metaphor where one signifier substitutes for another signifier.[32] In displacing the meaning and emotional response from one memory to the other, the manifest content serves to hide the true cause behind a symbolic substitution. The symptom thus has a rhetorical and poetic function since it relies on the role of symbolic association through the activation of the primary processes.

It is vital to realize that from Freud's perspective, we have to distinguish at least three different levels of symbolism. As we saw above, one level concerns the way our minds automatically equate different events and perceptions through the primary process of association. Here, correlation is confused with causation as the occurrence of two events at the same time and place is treated as an equivalence. Just as metaphors find similarities in two different things, the primary processes rely on treating different perceptions and memories as if they are the same thing.[33] This primary mode of symbolism is contrasted to the social mode of the symbolic order, where the relation between signifiers is predetermined by social consensus and tradition. As Lacan posits, we are born into a social order that is already structured by a set of symbolic signifiers and relations.[34] Freud adds that on a third level of symbolism, both the social and personal association between different events is distorted through a process of substitution, which he will later call repression:

> Symbols are formed in this way normally as well. A soldier will sacrifice himself for a piece of coloured cloth on a pole, because it has become the symbol of his native country; and no one considers this neurotic. But a hysterical symbol behaves differently. The knight who fights for a lady's glove *knows,* in the first place, that the glove owes its importance to the lady; and, secondly, his worship of the glove does not in the least prevent him from thinking of the lady and serving her in other ways. But the hysteric who is reduced to tears by *A* is unaware that this is because of the association *A-B,* and *B* itself plays no part whatever in his mental life. In this case the symbol has taken the place of the thing completely. (407)

In saying that the symbol has taken the place of the thing, Freud is indicating that in the formation of a neurotic symptom, one of the signifiers in the signifying relationship has been replaced through substitution, and it is this process that defines repression and the possibility of the unconscious: "We can sum the matter up by saying that *A* is compulsive and *B* repressed (at least from consciousness). Analysis has revealed the surprising fact that for every compulsion there is a corresponding repression, that for every excessive irruption into consciousness there is a corresponding amnesia" (407). A key then to understanding the psychoanalytic theory of the unconscious is to recognize this symbolic structure and the ways that one memory can substitute for another memory.[35]

In contrast to neuroscience and other contemporary models of the human mind, Freud does not define the unconscious by the fact that we are not aware of how the mind functions or that the content remains unknown; rather, the unconscious is derived from repression, and so the central issue is why do we repress certain thoughts and feelings.[36] Freud's initial response to this question is that symbolic substitution is triggered by the distressing nature of our own thoughts and feelings: "Repression is exclusively brought to bear on ideas that, firstly, arouse a distressing affect (unpleasure) in the ego, and that, secondly, relate to sexual life" (408). In other words, the reason why we hide things from ourselves is that these thoughts and feelings make the ego uncomfortable, and one of the things that causes the most discomfort is the presence of thoughts and memories of a sexual nature.[37] While Freud at this point does not develop his theory of the moral conscience in the form of the super-ego, it is clear that it is through the internalization of social norms and laws that sexuality becomes a source of unpleasure. Since the ego wants to maintain an ideal self-image, any feelings of guilt and shame have to be repressed through the creation of a symbolic substitute.[38]

In order to understand psychoanalytic theory and practice, it is therefore necessary to see the relations among symbolism, repression, social norms, and the super-ego. Furthermore, Freud highlights how what triggers the activation of the primary processes in the unconscious is the failure of the ego to control our thinking:

> Thus it is the business of the ego to permit no release of affect, since this would at the same time permit a primary process. Its best instrument for this purpose is the mechanism of attention. If a cathexis which releases unpleasure were able to escape attention, the ego's intervention would come too late. And this is precisely what happens in the case of the hysterical proton pseudos [first lie]. Attention is focused on perceptions, which are the normal occasions for the release of unpleasure. But here it is not a perception but a memory-trace which unexpectedly releases unpleasure, and the ego discovers this too late. It has permitted a primary process, because it did not expect one. (415–416)

Freud defines hysteria here as the failure of the ego to block affect, and this lapse is due to the fact that while the ego is centered on perceiving the external world, memories of displeasure are allowed to emerge. It is interesting that he calls this process a lie because it appears to be more of the ego's inability to anticipate an upsetting memory.[39]

Since repression will later be defined as the way people lie to themselves in order to avoid thinking about upsetting thoughts, this early theory of the first lie has to be coupled with what Freud has been saying about the process of removing particular memory associations from consciousness.[40] Moreover, it is important to stress that the unconscious and the primary processes are two very different concepts. As we have seen, repression can represent the use of primary processes, but this only occurs after an act of self-deception, which divides the subject between what has been conscious and what has replaced the memory of a conscious thought. Hallucinations, dreams, and delusions are conscious, but they can also be rendered unconscious through repression.

Since we retain very few memories of our first five years of life, we only know our infantile experience through a symbolic reconstruction made mostly out of representations and stories from others.[41] From this perspective, our past is a black hole filled in by retrospective knowledge. In fact, Freud insists that one of the important aspects of human sexuality is that knowledge gained in puberty is used to re-interpret past sexual experiences: "the retardation of puberty makes possible the occurrence of posthumous primary processes" (416). In other words, childhood sexuality only becomes traumatic after-the-fact when new knowledge is internalized.[42] Due to this lag between infantile sexual experiences and puberty, the divide between reality and knowledge is only a specific example of a more general divide between experience and understanding.

The Defensive Ego of Attention

For Freud, mediating the relationship between our knowledge and our reality is the ego's intentions and attention:

> Attention consists in the situation of expectation being established even in regard to perceptions that do not even partly coincide with wishful cathexes. For it has become important to send out a cathexis to meet all perceptions. Attention is biologically justified; the question is merely one of how to give the ego guidance as to which expectant cathexis it is to establish: and this purpose is served by the indications of quality. (418)

By claiming that attention is directed by concerns for quality, Freud is indicating that we only attend to things in relation to the pleasure principle. He also implies that the ego's perception of the external world is not a passive process since one's interest determines to what one is going to pay attention.[43]

Guided by the dictates of the pleasure principle, the ego is primarily a defensive structure motivated to avoid displeasure and to prevent the awareness of the primary process.[44] What then happens in hysteria is that the ego fails to control the subject's own mind, and so automatic thinking is allowed to emerge. As a derivative of the pleasure principle, the ego uses intentionality and attention to select what information becomes conscious, yet, in neurosis, this structure breaks down as excessively intense and painful ideas are able to emerge. Furthermore, if we think of the ego as primarily a defensive structure, then the solution to neurosis cannot be a strengthening of this internal agency; instead, what is needed is a way to confront the reality of both inner and outer life, and this form of judgment is centered on what Freud calls the reality principle.

The Reality Principle

In the *Project,* Freud first develops his theory of the reality principle in order to explain how one can move beyond the pleasure principle and the primary processes:

> The first of these arises if, while it is in a wishful state, it freshly cathects the memory of the object and then sets the process of discharge in motion, where there can be no satisfaction because the object is not present *really* but only as an imaginary idea. At an early stage it is not in a position to make this distinction, since it can only work on the basis of the sequence of analogous states between its neurones [i.e. on the basis of its previous experience that the cathexis of the object was followed by satisfaction]. (386)

The central idea here is that we have to learn how to distinguish between an image of past satisfaction and reality, but this distinction is at first impossible because our primary processes confuse past scenes of satisfaction with the perception of the external world.[45]

In order to establish the reality principle through the separation of memories from perceptions, Freud claims that it is necessary for the ego to inhibit the primary processes: "Accordingly, it is the inhibition brought about by the ego that makes possible a criterion for distinguishing between a perception and a memory" (388). As we will later see, it is problematic to locate this form of reality testing in the ego because the ego itself is a defensive structure guided by the dictates of the pleasure principle. However, the crucial idea for psychoanalysis is this need to access reality by countering the primary processes. Freud explains this conflict between the automatic primary processes and the reality principle in the following personal example: "For instance, *it* has happened to me that in the agitation caused by a great anxiety I have forgotten to make use of the telephone, which had been introduced into my house a short time before. The recently established path succumbed to the state of affect. The facilitation-that is to say, what was old-established won the day. Such forgetting involves the *loss* of the power of selection, of efficiency and of logic, just as happens in dreams" (414). Freud posits here that in the state of anxiety, his mind was taken over by the primary process of symbolic association, which is in conflict with the role of selection, efficiency, and logic in the reality principle. Furthermore, Freud reveals here how the primary processes can intervene in everyday life as anxiety pushes people to make hasty symbolic associations based on past experiences.[46]

Freud insists that it takes time to apply the reality principle, and this need for delay is lost when emotions dominate: "'Reflection' is an activity of the ego which demands time, and it becomes impossible when the affective level involves large quantities. Hence it is that where there is affect there is hastiness and a choice of methods similar to that made in the primary process" (415). In this opposition between the primary processes and the reality principle, immediate emotions are placed in conflict with the slow process of reality testing and thoughtful reflection.[47]

As an Enlightenment thinker, Freud defines reason as the ability to distinguish fact from fiction, and this principle of rationality not only structures his view of science, but it also defines his theory of the reality principle:

> The education and development of this original ego take place in states in which there is a repetition of the craving, in states of *expectation*. The ego learns first that it must not cathect the motor images (with consequent discharge), until certain conditions have been fulfilled on the perceptual side. It learns further that it must not cathect the wishful idea beyond a certain degree, because, if it does, it will deceive itself in a hallucinatory manner. If, however, it respects these two restrictions and turns its attention to the new perceptions, it has a prospect of attaining the desired satisfaction. (426–427)

As a defense against the primary processes, Freud defines the reality principle as a method for avoiding self-deception.[48] He adds that in order to learn to accept reality, we also have to avoid the pleasure principle's drive to escape all tension and unpleasure: "Unpleasure remains the sole means of education" (428). In pitting education against the pleasure principle, Freud reveals the difficulty in learning anything new or upsetting.

For Freud, the best way to resist the dictates of the primary processes and the pleasure principle is to transform our thoughts into speech:

"Thus, thought which is *accompanied by the cathexis of indications of thought-reality or of indications of speech* is *the highest and most secure form of cognitive thought-process"* (431). We can consider this argument privileging speech over thought as the initial justification for the psychoanalytic process of free association. As Lacan insists, the only tool of analysis is speech, and so it is necessary to determine what occurs when the thoughts of the primary process are turned into this mode of discourse.[49]

However, it has to be stressed that speech alone does not counter the pleasure principle because our usual way of speaking is driven by the defensive nature of the ego. To clarify what kind of speech is connecting to the reality principle, Freud differentiates between practical and theoretical thought: "It is interesting to observe how *practical* thought lets itself be directed by the biological rule of defence. In *theoretical* (cognitive and critical) thought, the rule is no longer observed. This is intelligible; for in purposive thinking it is a question of finding *some* path and those paths to which unpleasure attaches can be excluded, whereas in theoretical thinking *every* path has to be investigated" (440). In declaring that every path of thought has to be examined, Freud opens up the door for free association and a form of reason that suspends bias. In other words, analytic practice is based on the modern idea of science, which Descartes defines as the suspension of prejudice by following truth wherever it leads.[50] Moreover, we see here how modern democratic free speech finds its home in psychoanalysis.

Notes

1. Freud, Sigmund. "Project for a scientific psychology (1950 [1895])." *The Standard Edition of the Complete Psychological Works of Sigmund Freud, Volume I (1886-1899): Pre-Psycho-Analytic Publications and Unpublished Drafts*. 1966. 281–391.
2. Meyer, Jan, and Ray Land. *Threshold concepts and troublesome knowledge: Linkages to ways of thinking and practising within the disciplines*. Edinburgh: University of Edinburgh, 2003.

3. Freud, Sigmund. "Beyond the pleasure principle." *The Standard Edition of the Complete Psychological Works of Sigmund Freud, Volume XVIII (1920-1922): Beyond the Pleasure Principle, Group Psychology and Other Works*. 1955. 1–64.
4. Ragland, Ellie. *Essays on the pleasures of death: From Freud to Lacan*. Routledge, 2013.
5. Samuels, Robert. *Freud for the twenty-first century: The science of everyday life*. Springer, 2019.
6. Freud, Sigmund. "Formulations on the two principles of mental functioning." *The Standard Edition of the Complete Psychological Works of Sigmund Freud, Volume XII (1911-1913): The Case of Schreber, Papers on Technique and Other Works*. 1958. 213–226.
7. Descartes, René. *Discourse on method and meditations on first philosophy*. Hackett Publishing, 1999.
8. Malcolm, Norman. "Dreaming and skepticism." *The Philosophical Review* 65.1 (1956): 14–37.
9. Occhionero, Miranda, and Piercarla Cicogna. "Phenomenal consciousness in dreams and in mind wandering." *Philosophical Psychology* 29.7 (2016): 958–966.
10. Freud, Sigmund. *Totem And Taboo: Some Points of Agreement between the Mental Lives of Savages and*. Routledge, 2013.
11. Freud, Sigmund. "Remarks on the theory and practice of dream-interpretation." *The Standard Edition of the Complete Psychological Works of Sigmund Freud, Volume XIX (1923-1925): The Ego and the Id and Other Works*. 1961. 107–122.
12. Chaitin, Gilbert D. *Rhetoric and culture in Lacan*. Cambridge University Press, 1996.
13. Lacan, Jacques, Alan Sheridan, and Malcolm Bowie. *The agency of the letter in the unconscious or reason since Freud*. Routledge, 2020.
14. Johnston, Adrian, and Catherine Malabou. *Self and emotional life: Philosophy, psychoanalysis, and neuroscience*. Columbia University Press, 2013.
15. Malmberg, Bertil. *Structural linguistics and human communication: An introduction into the mechanism of language and the methodology of linguistics*. Vol. 2. Springer Science & Business Media, 2012.
16. Ellmann, Maud. *The Nets of Modernism: Henry James, Virginia Woolf, James Joyce, and Sigmund Freud*. Cambridge University Press, 2010.

17. Samuels, Robert. *Psychoanalyzing the politics of the new brain sciences.* Springer, 2017.
18. Mills, Jon. "Lacan on paranoiac knowledge." *Psychoanalytic Psychology* 20.1 (2003): 30.
19. Fink, Bruce. *The Lacanian subject: Between language and jouissance.* Princeton University Press, 1997.
20. Riviere, Joan. "On the genesis of psychical conflict in earliest infancy." *International Journal of Psycho-Analysis* 17 (1936): 395–422.
21. Segal, Hanna. "Phantasy and reality." *International Journal of Psycho-Analysis* 75 (1994): 395–401.
22. Benvenuto, Bice. *Once upon a Time: The Infant in Lacanian Theory 1.* Routledge, 2018.
23. Lacan, Jacques, Alan Sheridan, and Malcolm Bowie. "The function and field of speech and language in psychoanalysis." *Écrits.* Routledge, 2020. 33–125.
24. Lacan, Jacques. "The seminar of Jacques Lacan: Book VIII: Transference: 1960-1961." (2011).
25. Benjamin, Jessica. *The bonds of love: Psychoanalysis, feminism, and the problem of domincation.* Pantheon, 2013.
26. Makari, George, J. "A history of Freud's first concept of transference." *International review of psycho-analysis* 19 (1992): 415–432.
27. Freud, Sigmund. "Remembering, repeating and working-through (Further recommendations on the technique of psycho-analysis II)." *The Standard Edition of the Complete Psychological Works of Sigmund Freud, Volume XII (1911-1913): The Case of Schreber, Papers on Technique and Other Works.* 1958. 145–156.
28. Leider, Robert J. "Analytic neutrality—a historical review." *Psychoanalytic Inquiry* 3.4 (1983): 665–674.
29. Freud, Sigmund, and Joseph Breuer. *Studies in hysteria.* Penguin, 2004.
30. Freud, Sigmund. "Fragment of an analysis of a case of hysteria (1905 [1901])." *The Standard Edition of the Complete Psychological Works of Sigmund Freud, Volume VII (1901-1905): A Case of Hysteria, Three Essays on Sexuality and Other Works.* 1953. 1–122.
31. Dor, Joël. *Introduction to the reading of Lacan: The unconscious structured like a language.* Other Press, LLC, 1998.
32. Lacan, Jacques. *The other side of psychoanalysis.* Vol. 17. WW norton & Company, 2007.

33. Kovecses, Zoltan. *Metaphor: A practical introduction.* Oxford University Press, 2010.
34. Miller, Jacques-Alain, ed. *The Seminar of Jacques Lacan: Book 1: Freud's Papers on Technique 1953-1954.* CUP Archive, 1988.
35. Freud, Sigmund. "Repression." *The Standard Edition of the Complete Psychological Works of Sigmund Freud, Volume XIV (1914-1916): On the History of the Psycho-Analytic Movement, Papers on Metapsychology and Other Works.* 1957. 141–158.
36. Solms, Mark. ""The unconscious" in psychoanalysis and neuroscience: An integrated approach to the cognitive unconscious." *The Unconscious.* Routledge, 2016. 30–50.
37. Brenner, Charles. "The nature and development of the concept of repression in Freud's writings." *The Psychoanalytic Study of the Child* 12.1 (1957): 19–46.
38. Freud, Sigmund. "The ego and the id (1923)." *TACD Journal*17.1 (1989): 5–22.
39. Freud, Sigmund. "The aetiology of hysteria." *The Standard Edition of the Complete Psychological Works of Sigmund Freud, Volume III (1893-1899): Early Psycho-Analytic Publications.* 1962. 187–221.
40. Boag, Simon. "Realism, self-deception and the logical paradox of repression." *Theory & Psychology* 17.3 (2007): 421–447.
41. Peterson, Carole, Andrea Smorti, and Franca Tani. "Parental influences on earliest memories." *Memory* 16.6 (2008): 569–578.
42. Faimberg, Haydée. "A plea for a broader concept of Nachträglichkeit." *The Psychoanalytic Quarterly* 76.4 (2007): 1221–1240.
43. Freud, Sigmund. "Some elementary lessons in psycho-analysis." *The Standard Edition of the Complete Psychological Works of Sigmund Freud, Volume XXIII (1937-1939): Moses and Monotheism, An Outline of Psycho-Analysis and Other Works.* 1964. 279–286.
44. Freud, Anna. *The ego and the mechanisms of defence.* Routledge, 2018.
45. Freud, Sigmund. "Negation." *Organization and pathology of thought: Selected sources.* Columbia University Press, 1951. 338–348.
46. Compton, Allan. "A study of the psychoanalytic theory of anxiety. I. The development of Freud's theory of anxiety." *Journal of the American Psychoanalytic Association* 20.1 (1972): 3–44.
47. Deigh, John. "Emotions: the legacy of James and Freud." *The International Journal of Psychoanalysis* 82.6 (2001): 1247–1256.

48. Samuels, Robert. “Science and the reality principle.” *Freud for the twenty-first century*. Palgrave Pivot, Cham, 2019. 5–16.
49. Lacan, Jacques, Alan Sheridan, and Malcolm Bowie. “The function and field of speech and language in psychoanalysis.” *Écrits*. Routledge, 2020. 33–125.
50. Samuels, Robert. “Logos, global justice, and the reality principle.” *Zizek and the rhetorical unconscious*. Palgrave Macmillan, Cham, 2020. 65–86.

3

Neuroscience and the Repression of Psychoanalysis

In the last chapter, I defined the central concepts of psychoanalysis, which I will now further elaborate by comparing these core ideas to how they have been often misunderstood by certain scholars in the field of neuroscience. In reading closely Mark Solms' *The Hidden Spring: A Journey to the Source of Consciousness*, I endeavor to reveal the limits of combining psychoanalysis with neuroscience.[1] One of my main points is to reveal how psychoanalysis offers a more truthful and realistic understanding of consciousness in comparison to the new brain sciences.

Natural Feelings

One of the first moves that Solms makes in his effort to explain human consciousness and the relation between neuroscience and psychoanalysis is to argue that feelings are natural and a key aspect of consciousness: "This requires me to convince you that feelings are part of nature, that they are not fundamentally different from other natural phenomena, and that they do something within the causal matrix of things. Consciousness, I will demonstrate, is about feeling, and feeling, in turn, is about how

R. Samuels, *(Mis)Understanding Freud with Lacan, Zizek, and Neuroscience*, The Palgrave Lacan Series, https://doi.org/10.1007/978-3-031-13327-5_3

well or badly you are doing in life. Consciousness exists to help you do better" (3–4). In equating consciousness to human emotions, Solms seeks to prove that the pleasure principle defines our awareness, and since he wants to derive feelings of pleasure and pain from nature and evolution, he is able to base human subjectivity on biological determinism.[2]

The initial problem with this formulation is that as Freud argues in his *Project for a Scientific Psychology*, the first way that humans seek to satisfy the pleasure principle is by hallucinating a previous scene of satisfaction. Through this act of mental imagination, we are able to break free from the constraints of reality and biology. Moreover, psychoanalysis explains the origin of consciousness through a fundamental confusion between perception and memory coupled with an automatic process of symbolic association, and it is this human ability to imagine a false reality that produces a gap between our minds and material reality.

This theory of hallucination through the primary processes, then, provides the key to answering the fundamental question of how we move from the physical brain to the mental mind.[3] As we shall see, for Solms, it is the biology of feelings derived from natural selection that provide the missing link, but this solution goes against both psychoanalysis and our everyday experience. Since we have the ability to imagine things that do not exist, we are not tied to the reality principle, evolutionary development, or biological determinism. Our minds give us a certain level of freedom and self-determination, even when we are not in control of our own thinking.[4]

One of the results of rejecting the psychoanalytic theory of consciousness is that the human mind can be equated with the brains of other animals: "Since the cerebral cortex is the seat of intelligence, almost everybody thinks that it is also the seat of consciousness. I disagree; consciousness is far more primitive than that. It arises from a part of the brain that humans share with fishes" (4). In equating human consciousness and feelings with parts of a fish's brain, Solms makes it easier to combine psychoanalysis and neuroscience as he also justifies the use of experiments on animals in order to explain human psychology.[5]

From a psychoanalytic perspective, we need to insist that humans and animals experience feelings in a much different way since as Freud stresses in his *Project*, human feelings are always being displaced through symbolic substitution and association (the primary processes).[6] Moreover, human emotions are affected by culture and other social forces, and so it makes little sense to explain human consciousness and emotion through the examination of other animals, and yet, this is precisely what Solms does: "Many readers will be horrified by the animal research findings I report here, precisely because they show that other animals feel just as we do. All mammals are subject to feelings of pain, fear, panic, sorrow and the like" (4). Although it is possible to find basic emotional responses in different animals, the complexity and variability of human feelings means that we need to separate the reflexes located in the brains of other animals from the emotions circulating in the human mind and social communication.[7] Moreover, since humans are less controlled by instincts than other animals, biological determinism is constantly being subverted by the diversity of human pleasure.[8] In fact, Freud's initial theories concerning human sexuality reveal that unlike other animals, our desires are open to constant displacement and substitution.[9] Ultimately, from a psychoanalytic perspective, anything can be the object of sexual satisfaction because humans are perverse. To reject this theory of sexuality is to reject psychoanalysis itself.

An Imaginary Unity

As I have been arguing, psychoanalysis provides a realistic understanding of human consciousness and emotions because it recognizes the roles played by mental imagination, social influences, and sexual perversion, and yet Solms wants to repress these defining aspects of analysis in order to derive human consciousness from natural feelings shared by other animals. In ignoring Freud's key concepts, Solms is able to provide an imaginary unification of psychoanalysis and neuroscience: "It could be said that what unites us is that we have built, sometimes unwittingly, upon the abandoned foundations that Freud laid for a science of the mind that prioritises feelings over cognition. (Cognition is mostly unconscious.)" (4–5). This claim that Freud privileged feelings over cognition is not only incorrect, but it also reveals Solms' profound misunderstanding of psychoanalysis and the human condition. The first thing to be stressed here is that from Freud's perspective, emotions are a form of cognition, and so it makes no sense to oppose them to symbolic thought.[10] As indirect and unintentional responses, emotions are always based on the cognitive interpretation of particular social or natural events. Even the biological response of anxiety has to be triggered by an external cue, which itself is defined on a cognitive and social level.[11]

The other major misunderstanding that Solms repeats is the notion that most of consciousness is unconscious. What he misses in this common misinterpretation is Freud's fundamental theory that the unconscious is derived from repression, and so just because we are not directly aware of something does not make our lack of awareness unconscious. Experiences can be preconscious or outside of consciousness, but when we say that a certain mental event is unconscious, we imply that a human subject has hidden a thought or feeling from self-awareness.[12] The unconscious therefore requires a division of subjectivity between the part that knows and the part that does not know. Furthermore, repression is driven by the desire to escape feelings of shame, guilt, fear, and anxiety, and so it does serve to satisfy the pleasure principle but only through a process of self-deception. Unfortunately, many psychologists and neuroscientists repress this theory of repression as they equate the unconscious with a lack of conscious awareness.[13]

Solms is therefore able to unify psychoanalysis and neuroscience by eliminating the meaning of all of Freud's basic concepts. In fact, we can think of his process of interpretation as an example of the primary processes through his use of association, substitution, and displacement. By claiming that minds are brains, he takes two different things and equates them together, which enables him the ability to displace the meaning of one object onto the other.[14] As a symbolic metaphor, the equivalence of the mind and the brain enables understanding at the cost of misunderstanding since attributes of one entity are displaced onto the other.[15] Of course, Solms does not examine his own rhetoric because his entire project tends to repress the symbolic aspects of thoughts and emotions.

One way that this repression of symbolic cognition is achieved is by turning to a behavioralist theory of conditioning: "For example, when the trigger of an involuntary behaviour is paired repeatedly with an artificial stimulus, then the artificial stimulus will come to trigger the same involuntary response as the innate stimulus" (11–12). Just as behavioralists like Skinner sought to shape human reactions by placing thought in an excluded black box, Solms affirms that like other animals, human reactions are defined by linking a reflex to particular cue or trigger.[16] However, as I pointed out above, humans are able to transcend simple conditioning because they have mental autonomy and open instincts. Also, the things that trigger our responses are often indirect, complex, symbolic, and social.

The Computer Brain

Like many other contemporary brain scientists, Solms tends to equate the mind with the brain and the brain with computers.[17] This rhetorical combination of two metaphors allows him to see human consciousness as an informational processing machine: "the mind (construed as information processing) is a function rather than a structure. On this view, the 'software' functions of the mind are implemented by the 'hardware' structures of the brain, but the same functions can be implemented equally well by other substrates, such as computers" (12). While Solms and others may want to compare the human mind with a computer, it is important to realize that computers, like fish and drooling dogs, do not actually think.[18] Although, you may be able to program a computer and train a dog, they do not have the type of mental autonomy that Freud ascribes to the primary processes. In fact, in a book dedicated to defining the essence of consciousness, it is interesting that Solms basically leaves thought out of the picture.

In equating the human mind with the brains of other animals and the information processing of computers, Solms excludes the very things that makes us human.[19] For instance, in the following passage, the human mind is represented as being centered on encoding, classifying, and storing information: "Thus, both brains and computers perform memory functions (they encode and store information) and perceptual functions (they classify patterns of incoming information by comparing them with stored information) as well as executive functions (they execute decisions about what to do in response to such information)" (12). This description leaves out the human ability to imagine things that do not exist and to interpret experience in a complex, ambivalent, and ambiguous way. As Freud presents in his *Project*, thought itself is indirect, irrational, and unintentional at its core. Furthermore, our perceptions are always filtered through a symbolic memory network with the processes of association, substitution, and displacement.

While Freud examined the essence of symbolic thought through his analysis of his own dreams, Solms' seeks to interpret dreams as merely an extension of consciousness: "Dreaming, after all, is nothing but a paradoxical intrusion of consciousness ('wakefulness') into sleep" (16). This explanation adds nothing to our understanding of dreams as it eliminates the symbolic dimension of Freud's theory.[20] It is therefore no surprise that Solms can combine neuroscience with psychoanalysis since he simply erases the content of Freud's theories and analytic practice itself.

Like many other brain scientists, Solms is bent on reducing complex cognitive processes to their biological and evolutionary foundations:[21]

> Because REM sleep arises from the cholinergic brainstem, an ancient and lowly part of the brain far from the majestic cortex where all the action of human psychology presumably takes place, he added that dreaming could not possibly be motivated by wishes; it was 'motivationally neutral'. Therefore, according to Hobson, Freud's view that dreams were driven by latent desires must be completely wrong. (21)

The argument here is that since the parts of the brain that are activated during dreaming belong to an early stage of animal evolution, Freud's theory that dreams are determined by wishes must be false. In other words, our primary processes are not driven by the pleasure principle or our symbolic memory system; instead, dreams are just the random firing of neurons void of any content or meaning.[22] There is thus an underlying nihilism to this discourse since the main effect is to render meaning and interpretation irrelevant. We are simply animal-machines programmed by natural selection and triggered through environmental cues.[23]

The Pleasure Principle Revised

As Solms eliminates issues of individual desire and cognition from his understanding of the human mind, he also develops a non-psychoanalytic conception of the pleasure principle. For instance, in the following passage, he reviews several current conceptions of human motivation:

> If there is one part of the brain that might be considered responsible for 'wishes', it is the mesocortical-mesolimbic dopamine circuit. It is anything but motivationally neutral. Edmund Rolls (and many others) calls this circuit the brain's 'reward' system. Kent Berridge calls it the 'wanting' system. Jaak Panksepp calls it the SEEKING system – and foregrounds its role in the function of foraging. This is the brain circuit responsible for 'the most energised exploratory and search behaviours an animal is capable of exhibiting'. It is also the circuit that drives dreaming. (27–28)

In this re-introduction of desire into dreaming, Solms stresses how the brain's reward systems are derived from animal behavior. Although, it is difficult to know if other animals do actually dream, what we do know is that humans are the only animals that imagine alternatives to reality through the use of the symbolic primary processes.[24] After all, only humans have complex symbol systems where one sign can represent multiple and conflicting references. In fact, one of Freud's great insights was to see how our minds have an automatic poetic function that enables imagination through the rhetorical manipulation of memory-representations. Not only did Freud argue that the primary processes treat words as things and things as words, but his analysis of dreams, jokes, symptoms, delusions, and fantasies is centered on a linguistic approach to human perception and cognition.[25] From this perspective, consciousness is the result of rhetorical representations.

Unfortunately, Solms has little to say about symbolism, rhetoric, or linguistics, other than the fact that there is a distinction between the manifest and latent content of subjective experiences. In fact, he defines psychoanalysis in the following manner:

> Its fundamental assumption was that manifest (nowadays called 'explicit' or 'declarative') subjective phenomena have latent (nowadays called 'implicit' or 'non-declarative') causes. That is, Freud argued that the erratic train of our conscious thoughts can be explained only if we assume implicit intervening links of which we are unaware. This gave rise to the notion of latent mental functions and, in turn, to Freud's famous conjecture of 'unconscious' intentionality. (32)

This passage is Solms at his most psychoanalytic, but once again, he fails to separate the theory of the unconscious from the primary processes. By focusing on the unconscious intentionality derived from the implicit missing links of associated ideas, he avoids the issue of why these links are missing in the first place. There is thus an important distinction that has to be made between the repression of unwanted feelings and thoughts and the way our stream of consciousness is shaped by the association of ideas in a network of substitutions and displacements. When you eliminate the causes of repression, you end up with a purely mechanical model that eliminates human subjectivity.

At one point, Solms does highlight Freud's theory of repression, but it is presented in a confused way and then later removed from consideration:

> He observed that patients adopted a far-from-indifferent attitude to their inferred unconscious intentions; it appeared to be more a matter of being unwilling rather than unable to become aware of them. He called this tendency variously 'resistance', 'censorship', 'defence' and 'repression', and observed that it prevents emotional distress. This in turn revealed the pivotal role that feelings play in mental life, how they underpin all sorts of self-serving biases. (32)

At first glance, this definition of the role of repression in creating the unconscious does appear to match Freud's theory; however, he does not include the role of guilt and shame in motivating the individual to repress certain material.[26] By simply connecting the unconscious material to feelings, the content of the unconscious and the target of the censorship is avoided.

Instead of stressing the ethical and moral roots of repression, Solms emphasizes the connection between unconscious material and bodily needs: "He concluded that what ultimately underpinned feelings were bodily needs; that human mental life, no less than that of animals, was driven by the biological imperatives to survive and reproduce. These imperatives, for Freud, provided the link between the feeling mind and the physical body" (33). What is missing from this explanation of psychoanalysis and unconscious content is the fundamental conflict between the social super-ego and the drives of the individual.[27]

Pleasure and the Unconscious

Even through Freud does base the pleasure principle on the biological process of homeostatic regulation, it is important to stress that the pleasure principle as a law of inertia is driven by the desire to use as little mental and physical energy as possible.[28] The result of this goal is to produce a biological urge that goes against biology. Instead of humans being guided by the pure drive for survival, we often engage in self-destructive acts in order to avoid both internal and external stimuli.[29] For examples, many addictive behaviors are shaped by the desire to escape feelings of guilt and shame, which results in using pleasure as a mode of release.[30] In this structure, not only are we escaping from the reality of our lives, thoughts, feelings, and memories, but we are also breaking with the fundamental imperative of natural selection. As a science of self-defeating behavior and thoughts, psychoanalysis is centered on the failures and distortions of self-preservation, and therefore, it makes little sense to try to base this field on purely biological or evolutionary grounds.[31] However, the desire for scientific certainty and social prestige often pushes people like Solms to repress the radical insights of psychoanalysis in order to return to biological determinism.[32]

In an example of this quest to reduce all of human thought and behavior to animal instincts programmed by evolution and located in particular brain regions, Solms returns to Freud's theories of the drives, the unconscious, and the pleasure principle:

> But here I had stumbled upon a major contradiction in Freud's classical conception: he had come to the conclusion that the 'id' was unconscious. This was one of his most fundamental conceptions about how the mind works. It was clear to me that the part of the brain that measures the 'demand upon the mind for work in consequence of its connection with the body' – the part that generates what Freud called 'drives', which are synonymous with Panksepp's 'homeostatic affects' (which trigger his wishful SEEKING mechanism) – was located in the brainstem and hypothalamus. This is the part of the brain that obeys the 'pleasure principle'. But how can feelings of pleasure be unconscious? As we saw with Damasio's patient, drives such as hunger and thirst and the desire to void are felt. Of course they are. (48)

In turning to his conception of natural feelings, Solms is able to argue that consciousness and the pleasure principle must be determined through biological processes; however, once again, he confuses the unconscious with a lack of awareness as he reduces the pleasure principle to the function of homeostasis. In fact, Freud often posited that affects and desires are at first conscious, and they become unconscious when they are repressed because of their generation of unpleasure.[33] If one does not accept these fundamental definitions and distinctions, then the specificity of psychoanalysis is lost.

As Freud articulates in his *Project*, feelings are shaped by the primary processes, and they are often distorted in the same way as consciousness: since emotions can be generated through association, substitution, and displacement, they can be experienced as being excessive or nonsensical. Yet, Solms ignores this theory and equates emotions with the pleasure principle and the drives in the id: "Freud got the functional relationship between the 'id' (brainstem) and the 'ego' (cortex) the wrong way round, at least insofar as feelings are concerned. He thought the perceiving ego was conscious and the feeling id was unconscious. Could he have got his model of the mind upside down?" (49–50). While Freud did say that feelings can become unconscious through repression, he stressed how these emotions are often conscious, but their cause can be unconscious.[34] Moreover, the pleasure principle does work outside of consciousness as a basic biological drive, whereas the ego uses attention, intention, and selection to repress the primary processes.[35]

What is so interesting is that in a book dedicated to solving the riddle of what defines consciousness, Solms' often equates the human mind with the brains of other animals. This drive to confuse correlations with causation may be in part derived from the desire to justify the use of animal experimentation in neuroscience and pharmacology.[36] After all, if there are no major differences between human consciousness and the awareness of other animals, we can test our drugs and our theories by manipulating other species. Of course, what is lost in this process is what makes humans different, and as I have been arguing, psychoanalysis is the discipline that is best suited to determine this difference because it is based on understanding the symbolic nature of thoughts, feelings, actions, and social order.

We shall see in the following passage that Solms' privileging of animal research pushes him to repress psychoanalysis and the symbolic aspects of humanity:

> Antonio Damasio concurs: 'Decorticated mammals exhibit a remarkable persistence of coherent, goal-oriented behaviour that is consistent with feelings and consciousness.' Neonatally decorticate rats, for example, stand, rear, climb, hang from bars and sleep with normal postures. They groom, play, swim, eat and defend themselves. Either sex is capable of mating successfully when paired with normal cage mates. When they grow up, the females show the essentials of maternal behaviour, which, though deficient in some respects, allow them to raise pups to maturity. (55)

The first thing to stress in this discussion of animal behavior is that we have no evidence that other animals have the ability to imagine other possibilities or to hallucinate the satisfaction of their desires.[37] What we do know is that other animals are often preprogrammed by natural selection to behave in highly limited and predictable behaviors.[38] For example, the mating practices of these animals are often restricted, while huma show the ability to make any activity a source of sexual pleasure.[39] Finally, for most other animals, the father plays little or no role in caring for the offspring, and it should be obvious that the social hierarchies of even the most advanced non-human animals are rigid and contained.[40]

Are You Unconscious?

One of the more frustrating aspects of Solms' work is that at times he does appear to recognize the differences between humans and other animals, but at other times, he shows a total lack of understanding this difference, and one of the major reasons for this inconsistency is the way he defines consciousness and the unconscious. In a very telling passage, he reflects on his own self-understanding only to repress the fundamental concept of the unconscious: "Judging by my own case, being awake and responsive and having conscious experience are more or less the same thing. As far as I know, I am never awake and responsive but phenomenally unconscious" (58). Since Freud defines the unconscious through the process of repression, it should be clear that it occurs when someone is awake. Moreover, Freud's radical conception of consciousness is based in part on his theory of dreaming and the fact that when we are asleep, we are conscious of our hallucinations.[41] In fact, consciousness itself is a form of hallucination because it relies on treating internal mental representations as he perception of the external world. Perhaps neuroscientists and philosophers cannot solve the riddle of human consciousness because they do not want to accept this radical nature of thought.[42]

A stumbling block for other disciplines concerning the nature of consciousness is the confusion between intentionality and awareness. In contrast to Solms, Freud argues that the primary processes shaping consciousness are not intentional, while the intentionality of the ego results in the repression of the primary processes.[43] In other terms, we can be aware of unintentional thoughts, and what often happens with the addition of intentionality is that our attention is restricted to what satisfies the dictates of the pleasure principle through repression.[44] In the following passage, we see how Freud's theories are reversed:

> Most of moment-to-moment psychological life must occur through nonconscious means if it is to occur at all [...] To consciously and wilfully regulate one's own behaviour, evaluations, decisions, and emotional states requires considerable effort and is relatively slow. Moreover, it appears to require a limited resource that is quickly used up, so conscious selfregulatory acts can only occur sparingly and for a short time. On the other hand,

> the non-conscious or automatic [psychological processes ...] are unintended, effortless, very fast, and many of them can operate at any given time. Most important, they are effortless, continually in gear guiding the individual safely through the day. (81–82)

The main problems with this conception of consciousness is that it equates the unconscious with a lack of intentionality instead of repression. Although, it is true that most of our physical and mental processes occur without our awareness, a lack of awareness is not what defines the unconscious.

It is important to stress that if a scientist does not define terms correctly, like consciousness and the unconscious, then it does not matter what technique is used to detect and explain that notion.[45] For example, in the following passage, Solms refers to an experiment that seeks to locate the unconscious in a particular brain region: "This shows that the negative and positive words must have been seen, read and understood unconsciously. Since reading with comprehension is an exclusively cortical function – a function of precisely the kind that the classical anatomists considered quintessentially 'mental' – we can only conclude that cortical functions are not inherently conscious" (83). This attempt to localize aspects of the unconscious is thus misguided because the unconscious is equated with a lack of awareness and not the process of repression. In fact, Freud created the category of the preconscious to point to mental content that was neither unconscious nor conscious.[46] As latent ideas that have the ability to become conscious, the preconscious ideas in the experiment discussed above do not help us to understand the nature of consciousness or the location of the unconscious.

Feelings, Consciousness, and the Pleasure Principle

While Solms seeks to base his theory of consciousness on the experience of feelings, he relates all emotions to the pleasure principle defined by the quest for self-preservation: "In short, pleasure and unpleasure tell you how you are doing in relation to your biological needs. Valence reflects the value system underwriting all biological life, namely that it is 'good' to survive and to reproduce and 'bad' not to do so" (96–97). This focus on biological survival and reproduction is in conflict with Freud's theories of the pleasure principle and sexuality. Early on in his work, Freud realized the human sexuality often went beyond the need for reproduction; in fact, he used the term perversion to point to the many deviations in the human sexual experience.[47] Freud also developed his theory of masochism to reveal the ways people find pleasure in suffering, and so it hard to say that psychoanalysis considers the pleasure principle as a drive for reproduction or self-preservation.[48] Furthermore, it is necessary to distinguish the emotional responses to internal and external stimuli from the stimuli themselves, and so the question of what it means to feel has to be examined.

Since Solms wants to equate feelings and consciousness with a biological cause shaped by evolution, he has to reduce the complexity of human drives and emotions: "If you swapped subjective redness with blueness there would be no consequences, but if you swapped the feeling of fear with separation distress (or hunger with urinary urgency), it would kill you" (98–99). A problem with definition of fear as it relates to self-preservation is that psychoanalysis often highlights how our fears are often irrational and inconsistent.[49] Since we fear things based on our particular psychopathology, it is incorrect to claim that humans and other animals experience fear and different emotions in the same way.

As I have been arguing, what allows Solms the ability to equate the mind with the brain and humans with other animals is his misunderstandings of the basic concepts of psychoanalysis. We see this problem in the following passage: "Emotional needs, too, can be managed automatically, by means of behavioural stereotypes such as 'instincts' (inborn survival and reproductive strategies, which Freud placed at the centre of his conception of the unconscious mind)" (99). In positing that the unconscious is shaped by the instinctual goals of survival and reproduction, Solms shows how far his discourse is from psychoanalysis. Not only does Freud's theory of the drives represent a break with natural instincts, but his key concept of the unconscious relies on the principle of repression.[50] In fact, Lacan claims that the status of the unconscious is ethical because it is centered on feelings of guilt and shame, which are themselves influenced by social and cultural norms.[51] Furthermore, guilt and shame require a certain level of human responsibility and freedom, since as Sartre argues, we can only be guilty if we can be responsible, and we can only be responsible if we have free will.[52]

In basing our drives and feelings on biological evolution, Solms follows many other brain scientists in the effort to deny free will, and without this concept of human autonomy, it is hard to see how psychoanalysis is possible.[53] In fact, Solms does at times return to the possibility of human freedom and responsibility: "What does 'voluntary' mean? It means the opposite of 'automatic'. It means subject to here-and-now choices. Choices can be made only if they are grounded in a value system – the thing that determines 'goodness' versus 'badness'. Otherwise, your responses to unfamiliar events would be random" (100). It is strange that Solms wants to ground our feelings of goodness and badness on values since most of his work seeks to base these responses on a purely automatic biological determinism. One possible reason for this contradictory discourse is that in his effort to combine neuroscience and psychoanalysis, he is forced to equate two opposing theories.

As the following passage presents, a central conflict between biological and psychoanalytic theories of human psychology concerns the issue of the difference between the instinct for survival and the drive for pleasure: "You decide what to do and what not to do on the basis of the felt consequences of your actions. This is the Law of Affect. Voluntary behaviour, guided by affect, thereby bestows an enormous adaptive advantage over involuntary behaviour: it liberates us from the shackles of automaticity and enables us to survive in unpredicted situations" (100–101). From the perspective of many evolutionary psychologists and neuroscientists, our actions are determined by the goal of survival; however, according to Freud's theory of the pleasure principle, the real driving force is our desire to escape any sense of mental tension.[54] The pleasure principle, then, conflicts with the reality principle because we privilege escape over the real, and the main way that we achieve this goal of release is by denying our own freedom and responsibility. Biological determinism is then a form of pleasure because it removes the tension caused by guilt and shame in eliminating free will and responsibility from human subjectivity.[55]

One of the clearest examples of Freud's concept of the pleasure principle is the experience of addictions. While on one level, we can say that the addicted person is seeking out a form of pleasure, the result is often self-destruction, which is in opposition to the evolutionary goal of self-preservation.[56] Although some would say that addicts are driven by purely biological forces, it should be clear that most people turn to drugs and other forms of escape in order to eliminate feelings of guilt, shame, and anxiety.[57] By removing free will and responsibility from addiction, the only solution becomes medication. Moreover, as I argue in *Psychoanalyzing the Politics of the New Brain Sciences*, evolutionary psychology and neuroscience often end up promoting the drugging of all forms of social and personal conflict.[58] After all, if our thoughts and behaviors are determined by biological forces, then the only solution can be a biological one.

Even though many neuroscientists now talk about epigenesis as a way of accounting for how the social environment can trigger the expression of specific genetic material, the main emphasis is usually still on how our minds and brains are driven by the laws of evolutionary biology.[59] In choosing biology over psychology and sociology, Solms empties psychoanalysis of its content from the inside. His ultimate investment in biology and evolution is evident in the following passage:

> We have started exploring affect via its bodily forms. This is because they provide the simplest examples, and no doubt they were also the first to appear in evolution. I think the 'dawn of consciousness' involved nothing more elaborate than valenced somatic sensations. What I want to show you now is that human emotions are complex versions of the same type of thing. They, too, are ultimately 'error' signals which register deviations from your biologically preferred states, which tell you whether the steps you are taking are making things better or worse for you. (102)

It should be clear that psychoanalysis would not exist if people only did things that were good for their own self-preservation; in fact, the psychoanalytic clinic proves that we cannot base consciousness or the pleasure principle on purely biological foundations. Not only do we often find pleasure in things that are bad for us, but we ignore emotional signals that seek to warn us against dangerous behaviors and self-destructive thoughts.[60]

As I have been arguing, the complexity of human thought, emotions, and behaviors demands that we do not equate humans with other animals, but Solms cannot resist making this type of correlation because he wants to ground psychoanalysis on what he considers to be scientific evidence:

> In what follows, when I switch back and forth from observations about animals to observations about humans, I am doing so deliberately. As Panksepp said when he was accused by colleagues of anthropomorphism towards animals: he would rather plead guilty to zoomorphism towards humans. The purpose of his experiments was to determine which brain structures and circuits reliably arouse the same affective responses, not only across individuals but also across species. When it comes to emotional affects, it turned out that seven of them can be reliably reproduced not only in all primates but also in all mammals, by stimulation of exactly the same brain structures and chemicals. (Many of them can be evoked in birds, too, and some in all vertebrates.) Mammals separated from birds about 200 million years ago; that is how old these emotions are. Still, since humans are mammals, in what follows I am going to focus on these seven types. As far as we know, these are the basic ingredients of the entire human emotional repertoire. All our myriad joys and sorrows appear to be the outputs of these seven systems, blending with each other and with higher cognitive processes. (103–104)

One could interpret this passage as indicating that all of our basic emotions are derived from natural selection and are equivalent to other animals, yet they become re-interpreted and re-purposed by "higher cognitive processes." However, Solms' goal is to base our understanding of human consciousness on these emotions, and so he is not just saying that the origins of our affective responses are biological; rather, he is positing that human consciousness is a product of natural selection, and in the process, he is eliminating free will, cultural influence, imagination, and abstract reason.[61]

One might ask why would someone who says he is invested in promoting psychoanalysis end up repressing this discipline, and the answer to this important question revolves around several factors. It is clear that a driving forces behind his text is that he wants to argue against the notion that psychoanalysis has no scientific basis. In turning to the theories of evolutionary psychology and neuroscience, he seeks to ground analysis in an accepted form of scientific empiricism. However, the problem with this approach is that it misrepresents both science and psychoanalysis. Like so many of the other brain scientists, Solms confuses science with scientism in his effort to produce a totalizing theory that equates scientific theories with reality.[62] As a new form of animism, scientism uses the primary processes to eliminate the difference between our thoughts and external reality.[63] Similar to a psychotic delusion, many brain scientists rely on biological determinism to argue that there is no difference between minds and brains, humans and animals, brains and computers, and nature and scientific theories. The generation of these equivalences rely on symbolic association, substitution, and displacement, but this use of rhetoric is itself repressed through a denial of the way language shapes our perceptions and consciousness. The only way, then, that humans can be equated with other animals is if you eliminate the way that complex symbolism mediates human thought, perception, memory, consciousness, behavior, and emotions.

As some of the new brain sciences seek to base all of human thought and culture on programs inherited through natural selection, all other disciplines are discredited since they are seen as not being scientific.[64] Yet, if we define science as the unbiased approach to reality using symbolic approximation, consensus, and probability, we can provide a better understanding of science as we show that other discourses can also be scientific. For example, what makes psychoanalysis scientific is that it takes a neutral approach to the content of free association as it produces theories centered on predicting defined patterns and responses. After all, Freud sought to find reason in unreason by tracing the role of symbolic association, substitution, displacement, and projection in human thought.[65] As a science of symbolic representation, psychoanalysis can provide testable hypotheses without relying on the reductive lens of biological determinism.

If the practice of psychoanalysis is to survive, it will necessary to both critique biological determinism and offer a better understanding of the essence of science itself. Since the biological model most often leads to pharmacological solutions, it is necessary to reveal the blind spots of this discourse. Furthermore, to show that psychoanalysis is indeed a science, its fundamental concepts have to be clarified as evidence is provided for the predictive power of this discipline. Although it is hard to perform randomized trials on psychoanalytic treatment, the key concepts can be tested if they are clearly understood.[66]

Nurture and Nature

In many forms of neuroscience and evolutionary psychology, a central debate concerns the conflict over nature and nurture. While psychoanalysis does not deny the importance of biology, evolution, and nature, Freud's theory emphasizes how instinctual forces are reshaped by experience, culture, history, and subjectivity. At times, Solms also recognizes this break from biological evolution, but his underlying theory usually returns to biological determinism. For instance, in the following discussion concerning human emotions, the variability of human feelings is both expressed and repressed:

> The major dissenting voice is that of Lisa Feldman Barrett. Again, the disagreement is attributable mainly to methodological differences. She focuses on self-reported emotions in humans and, not surprisingly, finds that there is enormous variability in how different people (and cultures) characterise and parse feelings. This does not disprove the fact that basic natural kinds lurk beneath the socially constructed surface. I will soon illustrate the mechanisms whereby such variability arises, but the short explanation is this: our reflexes and instincts provide rough-and-ready tools for survival and reproductive success, but they cannot possibly equip us adequately for the multiplicity of unpredicted situations and environments that we find ourselves in. We therefore need to adaptively supplement the innate responses through learning from experience. The fact that human beings do so with such ease is the major reason why, for better or worse, we came to dominate the world to the degree that we now do. (104)

Since we can redirect our drives based on our thoughts, experience, and culture, we are able to use biological programs in unexpected ways.[67] Our emotional responses, then, may have their roots in evolutionary forces, but the ways we supplement these instinctual responses transforms our feelings to such an extent that they separate from the consciousness of other animals: "The instinctual programmes that undergird actions in humans are typically so conditioned through learning that they are no longer recognisable as 'instinctual'. Yet instincts and reflexes are always there in the background" (104–105). The question remains of how important these background reflexes remain if human emotions have such diverse causes and effects?

Fundamentally, Solms wants to have it both ways as he continues to argue that our emotions and consciousness are purely instinctual and equivalent to other animals while he also reveals the many ways humans subvert this biological determinism:

> It is uncertain whether LUST should be classified as a 'bodily' or an 'emotional' affect. Some people even doubt that sexuality is a need. This is an excellent example of the difference between (unconscious) needs and the (conscious) affects they give rise to. When we engage in sexual acts, we are not usually trying to perform our biological duty. In fact, very frequently, we are hoping not to reproduce. As with sweet tastes versus energy supplies, what motivates us subjective beings is the pursuit of erotic pleasure, not reproductive success. That is, we are driven by feelings. But living organisms need to reproduce, at least on average. That is why sex became subjectively pleasurable in the first place, through natural selection. (105–106)

Since humans do not primarily use sex for reproduction, the evolutionary cause is broken, and yet, Solms has to return to biology and evolution to make psychoanalysis fit his version of science. Once again, by not tying the unconscious to repression, he displaces the fundamental meaning of psychoanalysis as he claims he is doing psychoanalytic work.

As Solms rightly points out, a driving force behind our emotions transcending biology is that we have to interact with other people to satisfy our needs:

> The main reason why 'emotional' needs are more difficult to meet than 'bodily' ones is that they typically involve other sentient agents, who have needs of their own; they are not mere substances like food and water. To

> satisfy sexual needs, therefore, we must supplement our innate knowledge with other skills, acquired through learning. This fact alone explains the wide variety of sexual activities that we indulge in, alongside the 'average' form that was bequeathed by natural selection. (106)

This reliance on working with the emotions and needs of others is one of the main sources for Freud's theory of transference, and yet Solms turns to this social factor in order to highlight the inter-subjective nature of sexuality.[68] The problem with this approach is that it rejects Freud's insight into how human sexuality is often centered on auto-erotism, which relies on a denial of the social and the needs of others.[69] Although psychoanalysis also highlights the role that culture plays in reshaping desire and the drives, the pleasure principle is centered on the release of tension and not on communication or social interaction.

This distinction between what is social and what is biological has to be supplemented by the anti-evolutionary aspects of human drives, which are themselves different from symbolic consciousness and unconscious repression. When we fail to make these distinctions, we rob psychoanalysis of the very things that make it important and different from other disciplines. For instance, in the following discussion of reflexes, instincts, and memories, we encounter a non-psychoanalytic use of psychoanalytic concepts: "Notice that learning does not erase reflexes and instincts; it elaborates, supplements and overrules them, but they are still there. Street lamps illuminate pathways by night, but they cannot get rid of the darkness altogether. The usual mechanism for updating long-term memories, 'reconsolidation' (which I'll describe in Chap. 10), doesn't apply to reflexes and instincts. That is because reflexes and instincts are not memories" (106). Freud would concur that memories and instincts are very different things, but the key distinction is between the primary processes and the pleasure principle. A basic Freudian principle is that once drives (instincts) are repressed into the unconscious, they become restructured through the primary processes. These symbolic associations, displacements, and substitutions make a break with biology, nature, material reality, and evolution. In turn, on another level, our desires are reshaped by culture and society through transference, identification, idealization, and morality. So while it may be true that learning (nurture) does not completely erase instincts (nature), the supplementation through repression, the primary processes, and social mediation makes these reflexes a secondary consideration.

From Theory to Practice

This turn to biology and neuroscience to ground psychoanalysis is part of the process of removing psychoanalysis from the ways we diagnose and treat mental disorders today. As Allan Horwitz describes in *DSM: A History of Psychiatry's Bible*, the desire to make psychiatry more scientific, respected, and profitable resulted in replacing psychoanalytic concepts with bio-chemical explanations.[70] Horwitz highlights how,

> Before the 1980s, psychiatric diagnoses were inextricable from the experiences of particular individuals. Clinicians viewed mental problems as being closely intertwined with people's psychosocial backgrounds and circumstances and therefore impossible to isolate from personal interpretations, identities, socialization, relationships, and life events. This view of mental illness sharply divided psychiatry from other medical specialties, which studied diseases with predictable courses and outcomes that were independent of particular individual lives. (2)

According to this history of the Diagnostic and Statistical Manual of Mental Disorders (DSM,) before 1980, psychoanalysis still played a major role in describing and explaining different mental pathologies, but Freudian theories were soon replaced by decontextualized medical descriptions of symptoms:[71]

> Since the DSM-III, however, psychiatric diagnoses have been considered comparable to organic diseases that "can and should be thought of as entities existing outside the unique manifestations of illness in particular men and women. Mental, as much as physical, diseases are discrete ailments with characteristic causes, prognoses, and outcomes. Their diagnoses stand apart from the singularity of the individual patient. (2)

What in part allowed for this move away from psychoanalysis in psychiatry and other forms of therapy was a growing desire to see mental issues as organic diseases.[72]

A side-effect, then, of Solms' discourse is that its focus on biological determinism feeds the drive to replace social and psychological interpretations with the natural sciences. Likewise, in moving away from the inner dynamics of individuals and the conflicts between society and the drives, the standardized diagnostic manual was able to repress psychoanalysis as it determined the economic and practical future of mental health treatment:

> The manual establishes which psychiatric conditions are taught in medical and other professional schools, determine eligibility for disability payments for patients and insurance compensation for providers, are targeted by pharmaceutical advertisements, become objects of psychiatric research, and shape public formulations of mental illness. It is also firmly embedded in the administrative apparatus of hospitals, private practices, the judicial system, and all other institutions that deal with mental disorder. Moreover, the DSM shapes the way individuals conceive of their own psychological problems. (3)

Due to a wide-range of social and individual incentives, it became highly desirable to replace psychoanalysis with a model based on medical diagnosis even when the new system failed to explain any of the causes for the symptoms and behaviors it was cataloging.[73]

Since the DSM broke it ties to Freudian theory, it was able to expand the number of diagnostic categories:

> Moreover, rates of DSM disorders appear to be rising at an alarming pace: studies conducted in the 1980s, 1990s, and 2000s show continuously growing numbers of individuals with these conditions. The use of DSM diagnoses thus makes it seem as if mental disorders are rampant in the population. Far from being a specialty that treats a small group of seriously disturbed people, psychiatry (and other mental health professions) is charged with a mission to confront a large and growing "public health epidemic" that threatens virtually everyone. Without exaggeration, a former president of the APA claims that "the DSM might just be the most influential book written in the past century." (5)

This constant expansion of diagnostic categories not only helped to provide new markets for mental health specialists and pharmaceutical companies, but it also provided a new way for individuals to see themselves. In fact, even before the turn to neuroscience and evolutionary psychology, the leaders of the American Psychiatric Association figured out that the best way to sell their new diagnostic categories was to model them on the scientific approach to medical diseases:

> Since its third edition, many psychiatrists have viewed the DSM as the product of improving empirical knowledge about mental disorder. They regard the first two editions as reflecting the unscientific or even anti-scientific views of eclectic American psychiatrist Adolf Meyer and psychoanalyst Sigmund Freud. After the DSM-III revolution in 1980, however, scientific evidence has served as the foundation of psychiatric diagnoses. Therefore, the evolution of the manual represents the triumph of "science over ideology": "The old psychiatry derives from theory, the new psychiatry from fact." (5–6)

In representing psychoanalysis as unscientific, the space was cleared for a new medical model of mental illness. From this perspective, Solms' attempt to combine psychoanalysis and neuroscience together is problematic since the repression of Freud's theory has been driven by the desire to replace analysis and theory with empirical methods borrowed from the natural sciences.[74]

It is vital to point out that this replacement of psychoanalysis was mainly driven by a set of political and economic interests:

> During the 1950s and 1960s, analytically oriented psychiatrists, who scorned the use of specific diagnoses organized by observable symptoms, dominated the organization. Consequently, the first two DSMs paid little attention to developing precise specifications of diagnostic criteria. After the 1960s, however, intense pressures developed from, among other sources, federal regulators, insurance companies, and medical schools to portray psychiatrists as doctors practicing medicine. (8)

The desire to increase the profits and prestige of psychiatrists and pharmaceutical companies helped to motivate this move from psychoanalysis to the medical sciences, which in turn was fed by insurance companies and governmental regulations.[75] In other words, the definition of mental illness and its treatment was not determined by an enhanced understanding of the mind; rather, various vested interests sought to cash in on a system that was not based on any underlying theory.

As Horwitz emphasizes, the changes in the DSM were often the result of a battle between clinicians and researchers:

> There are also clear intra-professional divisions regarding the role of diagnoses. In particular, researchers and clinicians use the DSM in distinct ways. Researchers require specific diagnoses to create homogeneous groups that can reveal the etiology, prognosis, and best treatments for the particular condition under study. Their definitions must be similar to those of others who study comparable phenomena. In contrast, clinicians must deal with the idiosyncrasies of particular clients. For them, diagnoses are practical tools, not the basis for standardized protocols. (9)

While researchers need clear diagnostic categories, analysts are more concerned about the specificity of each individual case. The way that this conflict was resolved was to give both sides what they wanted by standardizing diagnostic categories and multiplying them to such an extent that every individual could be covered. Moreover, since clinicians wanted to be re-imbursed by insurance companies that required defined diagnosis and treatment plans, they had to conform to a system in which they did not really believe.[76]

Horwitz adds that it was often the pharmaceutical industry that was fueling this drive for more standardized diagnostic categories:

> pharmaceutical companies have been intimately connected to diagnostic classification systems. Since the early 1970s, the Food and Drug Administration's (FDA) regulations have required the drug industry to market its products as treatments for particular DSM diagnoses. Drug companies are also a major source of income for departments of psychiatry in medical schools, psychiatric researchers, and the APA. The web of affiliations between the industry and the psychiatric profession is tight enough that nearly three-quarters of the members of the latest DSM task force had

> ties to drug companies. Moreover, pervasive drug advertisements are probably the most significant conduit of information to the general public about DSM diagnoses. (9)

Here we find the core of what I have called the Governmental University Medical Pharmaceutical Complex (GUMP).[77] The government forces drug companies to cater to particular diagnostic categories, while these same corporations fund university medical research and required drug trials. Meanwhile, the professional association that authors the diagnostic manual is shaped by pharmaceutical interests, and the individual psychiatrists increase their pay and prestige by invoking a medical and scientific approach to mental illness.

All of these intertwined incentives are further enabled by the desire of patients to receive a clear diagnosis that fortifies their identity and provides access to care and financial support: "Patients and their families sought them to obtain desired treatments, reimbursement for care, eligibility for government benefits, provision of special education resources, and explanations for distress" (10). Although it appears that everyone has a stake in the diagnostic bible, what is still unclear is if this system of diagnosis has any real validity or scientific value.

In fact, Horwitz reveals how there is little connection between the development and marketing of psychotropic drugs and a scientific understanding of different mental disorders:

> As later developments would show, almost all psychotropic drugs do not work specifically for particular DSM mental disorders. Nevertheless, declining tranquilizer sales, coupled with congressional pressure and the resulting FDA mandate, provided powerful reasons for the pharmaceutical industry to market its products as remedies for specific diseases. Biological psychiatrists, pharmaceutical companies, the FDA, and the NIMH all began to push a narrative centered on the specificity of diagnostic categories. "During the 1970s the major psychiatric disorders became defined as disorders of single neurotransmitter systems and their receptors, with depression being a catecholamine disorder, anxiety a 5HT disorder, dementia a cholinergic disorder, and schizophrenia a dopamine disorder," Healy explains. (10)

What we learn here is that the new brain sciences played a key role in propping up the pharmaceutical industry's need to match their medication with specific diagnostic categories; using the disease model from the medical sciences, university researchers and pharmaceutical interests promoted the idea that mental problems derived from chemical imbalances.[78]

In the battle between psychoanalytic treatment and medication, Big Pharma won by turning to scientific theories bent on discrediting Freud. Moreover, insurance companies enhanced their influence by dictating what treatments would be allowed for specific diagnosis:

> Between the mid-1960s and 1980, the percentage of patients using insurance to pay for outpatient psychotherapy rose from 38 to 68 percent. While patients had little concern with particular diagnostic categories, the third parties that increasingly paid for their treatment were coming to demand that it involve genuine diseases and not problems in living. Insurers were willing to fund only a specific number of visits for well-defined problems and cast an especially sharp eye on what could often be interminable psychoanalytic sessions. The nebulous DSM-II conditions poorly fit an insurance logic that would reimburse the treatment of only discrete diseases. (49–50)

Since the insurance companies would only support payments for specific diseases, and clinicians relied on insurance payments, the clinicians had to buy into a system that often went against their own beliefs and practices. In fact, as Horwitz documents, academic researchers, pharmaceutical corporations, and psychiatric institutions all dismissed the fundamental basis of psychoanalytic treatment:

> Another central distinction between practitioners and investigators is the role of clinical intuition. The particular insights and relationships therapists have with their patients are essential aspects of clinical practice. Indeed, the process of "transference," which involves the specific psychological dynamics in therapeutic encounters, is an essential aspect of analytic treatments. Researchers, however, strove to abolish the role of particular clinicians in defining any disorder. They regarded the dominant analytic therapeutic model as the offspring of such discredited practices as mesmerism or hypnotism. In their view, optimal practice would replace clinical

> insight with reliable diagnostic criteria grounded in observable symptoms and decision rules that do not depend on the personal characteristics of either patients or clinicians. (52)

In dismissing the key role of transference in the analytic process, researchers and other interested parties sought to eliminate psychoanalytic practice and theory and replace it with a purely abstract scientific discourse.

Defending the Science of Psychoanalysis

Since psychoanalysis has been discredited for not being empirical, it is important to examine if psychoanalysis is actually a science. As we saw in Solms' work, the turn to neuroscience and evolutionary psychology has been in part driven by a desire to provide clinicians with a more consistent and realistic theory and practice. This same drive for reliable data has also shaped some of the transformations of the DSM; however, as Horwitz insists, there is very little evidence that we can base most mental issues on biology: "Given the absence of known pathogens or objective tests for any mental disorder, the DSM-III diagnoses emerged in the only possible way: through a messy procedure marked by arguments, heated discussions, and, eventually, reluctant consensus" (58). In other words, a manual that sought to eliminate the social and the individual ended up being determined by the social negotiations of individuals because there really was no scientific foundation to its system.[79]

As a catalogue of discrete symptoms and behaviors, the DSM continues to be a set of descriptions lacking an underlying theory. Although Freud clearly divided different type of mental disorders based on their central mode of defense (projection, repression, denial), the desire to find an organic cause for most mental disorders has pushed the mental health system to rely on a fragmented list of disconnected manifestations. A return to Freud's fundamental concepts is thus necessary in order to clarify the theory and treatment of mental disorders because without a grounding in an integrated system, there is nothing to stop the destructive drugging of individuals and social discontent.

Notes

1. Solms, Mark. *The hidden spring: A journey to the source of consciousness.* WW Norton & Company, 2021.
2. Rose, Steven, Richard Charles Lewontin, and L. Kamin. "Not in our genes: Biology, ideology and human nature." *The Wilson Quarterly* 152 (1984).
3. Chalmers, David. "The hard problem of consciousness." *The Blackwell companion to consciousness* (2007): 225–235.
4. Samuels, Robert. "The Backlash Politics of Evolutionary Psychology: Steven Pinker's Blank Slate." *Psychoanalyzing the Politics of the New Brain Sciences.* Palgrave Pivot, Cham, 2017. 35–58.
5. Bourtchouladze, Rusiko. *Memories are made of this: How memory works in humans and animals.* Columbia University Press, 2002.
6. Żechowski, Cezary. "Theory of drives and emotions-from Sigmund Freud to Jaak Panksepp." *Psychiatr Pol* 51.6 (2017): 1181–1189.
7. Barrett, Lisa Feldman. *How emotions are made: The secret life of the brain.* Houghton Mifflin Harcourt, 2017.
8. Freud, Sigmund. "Instincts and their vicissitudes." *The Standard Edition of the Complete Psychological Works of Sigmund Freud, Volume XIV (1914-1916): On the History of the Psycho-Analytic Movement, Papers on Metapsychology and Other Works.* 1957. 109–140.
9. Freud, Sigmund. *Three essays on the theory of sexuality: The 1905 edition.* Verso Books, 2017.
10. Natsoulas, Thomas. "Freud and consciousness: V. Emotions and feelings." *Psychoanalysis and Contemporary Thought*14.1 (1991): 69–108.
11. Freud, Sigmund, James Strachey, and Alix Strachey. *Inhibitions, symptoms and anxiety.* New York: Norton, 1977.
12. Freud, Sigmund. "Repression." *The Standard Edition of the Complete Psychological Works of Sigmund Freud, Volume XIV (1914-1916): On the History of the Psycho-Analytic Movement, Papers on Metapsychology and Other Works.* 1957. 141–158.
13. Samuels, Robert. "Damasio's Error: The Politics of Biological Determinism After Freud." *Psychoanalyzing the Politics of the New Brain Sciences.* Palgrave Pivot, Cham, 2017. 9–33.

14. Crowther-Heyck, Hunter. "George A. Miller, language, and the computer metaphor and mind." *History of Psychology* 2.1 (1999): 37.
15. Maasen, Sabine. "Who is afraid of metaphors?." *Biology as society, society as biology: Metaphors*. Springer, Dordrecht, 1995. 11–35.
16. Delprato, Dennis J., and Bryan D. Midgley. "Some fundamentals of BF Skinner's behaviorism." *American psychologist* 47.11 (1992): 1507.
17. Rose, Nikolas, and Joelle M. Abi-Rached. *Neuro: The new brain sciences and the management of the mind*. Princeton University Press, 2013.
18. Searle, John. "Can computers think." *Minds, brains, and science* (1984): 28–41.
19. Harari, Yuval Noah. "Sapiens: a brief history of humankind by Yuval Noah Harari." (2018).
20. Freud, Sigmund, and James Strachey. *The interpretation of dreams*. New York: Gramercy Books, 1996.
21. Samuels, Robert. "Drugging Discontent: Psychoanalysis, Drives, and the Governmental University Medical Pharmaceutical Complex (GUMP)." *Psychoanalyzing the Politics of the New Brain Sciences*. Palgrave Pivot, Cham, 2017. 115–136.
22. Northoff, Georg. "Psychoanalysis and the brain–why did Freud abandon neuroscience?." *Frontiers in psychology* 3 (2012): 71.
23. Sahlins, Marshall David. *The use and abuse of biology: An anthropological critique of sociobiology*. University of Michigan Press, 1976.
24. Siegel, Jerome M. "Do all animals sleep?." *Trends in neurosciences* 31.4 (2008): 208–213.
25. Dor, Joël. *Introduction to the reading of Lacan: The unconscious structured like a language*. Other Press, LLC, 1998.
26. Rieff, Philip. *Freud: The mind of the moralist*. University of Chicago Press, 1979.
27. Freud, Sigmund. *Civilization and its discontents*. Broadview Press, 2015.
28. Ansermet, Jean-Philippe, Pierre Magistretti, and Francois Ansermet. "From the Principle of Inertia to the Death Drive: The Influence of the Second Law of Thermodynamics on the Freudian Theory of the Psychical Apparatus." *Frontiers in psychology* 11 (2020): 325.
29. Samuels, Robert. "Catharsis: The politics of enjoyment." *Zizek and the rhetorical unconscious*. Palgrave Macmillan, Cham, 2020. 7–31.
30. Flanagan, Owen. "The shame of addiction." *Frontiers in Psychiatry* 4 (2013): 120.

31. Menninger, Karl, A. "Psychoanalytic aspects of suicide." *International Journal of Psycho-Analysis* 14 (1933): 376–390.
32. Klahr, Carl N. "Science versus scientism." *Challenge: Torah Views on Science and Its Problems, eds. Aryeh Carmell and Cyril Domb,* (1976): 288–295.
33. Boag, Simon. "Freudian repression, the common view, and pathological science." *Review of General Psychology* 10.1 (2006): 74–86.
34. Turner, Jonathan H. "Psychoanalytic sociological theories and emotions." *Handbook of the sociology of emotions*. Springer, Boston, MA, 2006. 276–294.
35. Freud, Sigmund. *Group Psychology and the Analysis of the Ego*. Duke University Press, 2007.
36. Bennett, Allyson J., and Dario L. Ringach. "Animal research in neuroscience: a duty to engage." *Neuron* 92.3 (2016): 653–657.
37. Rilling, M. E., and J. J. Neiworth. "How animals use images." *Science Progress (1933-)* (1991): 439–452.
38. Samuels, Robert. "Damasio's Error: The Politics of Biological Determinism After Freud." *Psychoanalyzing the Politics of the New Brain Sciences*. Palgrave Pivot, Cham, 2017. 9–33.
39. Parker, G. A. "Sperm competition and the evolution of animal mating strategies." *Sperm competition and the evolution of animal mating systems* (1984): 1–60.
40. Raeburn, Paul. *Do fathers matter?: What science is telling us about the parent we've overlooked*. Scientific American/Farrar, Straus and Giroux, 2014.
41. Basch, Michael, Franz. "Perception, Consciousness, and Freud's "Project"." *Annual of Psychoanalysis* 3 (1975): 3–19.
42. Jones, Simon R., and Charles Fernyhough. "Rumination, reflection, intrusive thoughts, and hallucination-proneness: Towards a new model." *Behaviour Research and Therapy*47.1 (2009): 54–59.
43. Erdelyi, Matthew Hugh. "The unified theory of repression." *Behavioral and Brain Sciences* 29.5 (2006): 499–511.
44. Cohen, Aviva. "Franz Brentano, Freud's philosophical mentor." *The pre-psychoanalytic writings of Sigmund Freud*. Routledge, 2018. 88–100.
45. Legrenzi, Paolo, and Carlo Umiltà. *Neuromania: On the limits of brain science*. Oxford University Press, 2011.
46. Zepf, Siegfried. "The relations between language, consciousness, the preconscious, and the unconscious: Freud's approach conceptually updated." *The Scandinavian Psychoanalytic Review* 34.1 (2011): 50–61.

47. Freud, Sigmund. "Three essays on the theory of sexuality (1905)." *The standard edition of the complete psychological works of Sigmund Freud, volume VII (1901-1905): A case of hysteria, three essays on sexuality and other works.* 1953. 123–246.
48. Freud, Sigmund. "The economic problem of masochism." *The Standard Edition of the Complete Psychological Works of Sigmund Freud, Volume XIX (1923-1925): The Ego and the Id and Other Works.* 1961. 155–170.
49. Freud, Sigmund. *Obsessions and phobias.* Read Books Ltd, 2014.
50. Freud, Sigmund. "Instincts and their vicissitudes." *The Standard Edition of the Complete Psychological Works of Sigmund Freud, Volume XIV (1914-1916): On the History of the Psycho-Analytic Movement, Papers on Metapsychology and Other Works.* 1957. 109–140.
51. Soler, Colette, Esther Faye, and Susan Schwartz. *Lacan—The Unconscious Reinvented: The Unconscious Reinvented.* Routledge, 2018.
52. Sartre, Jean-Paul. *Being and nothingness: An essay in phenomenological ontology.* Citadel Press, 2001.
53. Harris, Sam. *Free will.* Simon and Schuster, 2012.
54. Suttie, Ian D. "Critical Review: METAPSYCHOLOGY AND BIOLOGY: Some criticisms of Freud's "Beyond the Pleasure Principle."." *Journal of Neurology and Psychopathology* 5.17 (1924): 61.
55. Samuels, Robert. "Catharsis: The politics of enjoyment." *Zizek and the rhetorical unconscious.* Palgrave Macmillan, Cham, 2020. 7–31.
56. Rado, Sandor. "The psychoanalysis of pharmacothymia (drug addiction)." *The Psychoanalytic Quarterly* 2.1 (1933): 1–23.
57. Kim, Eunhyang, and Eunyoung Koh. "Avoidant attachment and smartphone addiction in college students: The mediating effects of anxiety and self-esteem." *Computers in Human Behavior* 84 (2018): 264–271.
58. Samuels, Robert. "Drugging Discontent: Psychoanalysis, Drives, and the Governmental University Medical Pharmaceutical Complex (GUMP)." *Psychoanalyzing the Politics of the New Brain Sciences.* Palgrave Pivot, Cham, 2017. 115–136.
59. Robert, Jason Scott. *Embryology, epigenesis and evolution: Taking development seriously.* Cambridge University Press, 2004.
60. Vazire, Simine, and David C. Funder. "Impulsivity and the self-defeating behavior of narcissists." *Personality and social psychology review* 10.2 (2006): 154–165.

61. Samuels, Robert. "The Brain Sciences Against the Welfare State." *Psychoanalyzing the Politics of the New Brain Sciences*. Palgrave Pivot, Cham, 2017. 85–114.
62. Hacker, P. M. S. "Philosophy and scientism: What cognitive neuroscience can, and what it cannot, explain." *Scientism: The new orthodoxy* (2015): 97–115.
63. Samuels, Robert. "Conclusion: Science, Politics, Media, and the Virus." *Viral Rhetoric*. Palgrave Macmillan, Cham, 2021. 109–112.
64. Samuels, Robert. "The Backlash Politics of Evolutionary Psychology: Steven Pinker's Blank Slate." *Psychoanalyzing the Politics of the New Brain Sciences*. Palgrave Pivot, Cham, 2017. 35–58.
65. Westen, Drew. "The scientific legacy of Sigmund Freud: Toward a psychodynamically informed psychological science." *Psychological bulletin* 124.3 (1998): 333.
66. Westen, Drew. "The scientific legacy of Sigmund Freud: Toward a psychodynamically informed psychological science." *Psychological bulletin* 124.3 (1998): 333.
67. Hodgson, Geoffrey M. "Choice, habit and evolution." *Journal of Evolutionary Economics* 20.1 (2010): 1–18.
68. Samuels, Robert. "Transference and Narcissism." *Freud for the Twenty-First Century*. Palgrave Pivot, Cham, 2019. 43–51.
69. Kanzer, Mark. "Freud's uses of the terms "autoerotism" and "narcissism"." *Journal of the American Psychoanalytic Association* 12.3 (1964): 529–539.
70. Horwitz, Allan V. *DSM: A History of Psychiatry's Bible*. JHU Press, 2021.
71. Lane, Christopher. *Shyness: How normal behavior became a sickness*. Yale University Press, 2008.
72. Whitaker, Robert. "Anatomy of an epidemic: Psychiatric drugs and the astonishing rise of mental illness in America." *Ethical Human Psychology and Psychiatry* 7.1 (2005): 23.
73. Burston, Daniel. "Psychiatry and Anti-psychiatry: History, Rhetoric and Reality." *Eidos. A Journal for Philosophy of Culture* 2.2 (4) (2018).
74. Marquis, Andre, and Kathryn Z. Douthit. "Empiricism in psychiatry's post-psychoanalytic era: Contemplating DSM's" atheoretical" nosology." *Constructivism in the Human Sciences* 11.1/2 (2006): 32.
75. Goldacre, Ben. *Bad science: Quacks, hacks, and big pharma flacks*. McClelland & Stewart, 2010.

76. Cooper, Rachel. "What is wrong with the DSM?." *History of Psychiatry* 15.1 (2004): 5–25.
77. Samuels, Robert. "Drugging Discontent: Psychoanalysis, Drives, and the Governmental University Medical Pharmaceutical Complex (GUMP)." *Psychoanalyzing the Politics of the New Brain Sciences*. Palgrave Pivot, Cham, 2017. 115–136.
78. Moncrieff, Joanna. "The myth of the chemical cure." *The Myth of the Chemical Cure*. Palgrave Macmillan, London, 2008. 217–224.
79. Khoury, Bassam, Ellen J. Langer, and Francesco Pagnini. "The DSM: Mindful science or mindless power? A critical review." *Frontiers in psychology* 5 (2014): 602.

4

Moving from Freud's Five Principles to Lacan's Four Fundamental Concepts

As a way of clarifying what is at stake in (mis)understanding psychoanalysis, I will now turn to Lacan's *Four Fundamental Concepts of Psychoanalysis*, where he defines the central theories of the unconscious, repetition, transference, and the drives.[1] We shall see that a key to Lacan's interpretation is a conflation of the unconscious and the primary process and the replacement of the reality principle with the concept of repetition. Although Lacan does help to explain several of Feud's key ideas, he also displaces the meaning of other central notions.[2] Instead of simply rejecting or accepting Lacan's theories, then, I seek to develop a critical interaction with his interpretation of Freud's work.

The Unconscious and the Primary Processes

The first concept that Lacan examines in this seminar is the unconscious, but he makes a curious move by equating this notion with the theory of the subject and the way we are subjected to symbolic representations.[3] In fact, Lacan turns to the field of structural anthropology to posit that humans are born into a world that is already structured by a series of symbolic binary oppositions:[4]

R. Samuels, *(Mis)Understanding Freud with Lacan, Zizek, and Neuroscience*, The Palgrave Lacan Series, https://doi.org/10.1007/978-3-031-13327-5_4

> Most of you will have some idea of what I mean when I say--the unconscious is structured like a language. This statement refers to a field that is much more accessible to us today than at the time of Freud. I will illustrate it by something that is materialized, at what is certainly a scientific level, by the field that is explored, structured, elaborated by Claude Levi-Strauss, and which he has pinpointed in the title of his book, *La Pensee Sauvage*. Before any experience, before any individual deduction, even before those collective experiences that may be related only to social needs are inscribed in it, something organizes this field, inscribes its initial lines of force. This is the function that Claude Levi-Strauss shows us to be the truth of the totemic function, and which reduces its appearance--the primary classificatory function. Before strictly human relations are established, certain relations have already been determined. They are taken from whatever nature may offer as supports, supports that are arranged in themes of opposition. Nature provides-- must use the word--signifiers, and these signifiers organize human relations in a creative way, providing them with structures and shaping them. The important thing, for us, is that we are seeking here--before any formation of the subject, of a subject who thinks, who situates himself in it--the level at which there is counting, things are counted, and in this counting he who counts is already included. It is only later that the subject has to recognize himself as such, recognize himself as he who counts. (20)

The unconscious is thus considered here to be the effect of the pre-existing symbolic order. However, by saying that the unconscious is structured like a language, Lacan conflates three different things: the non-conscious symbolic organization of societies, the Freudian unconscious, and the primary processes. While Freud clearly defines the unconscious by the process of repression and the primary processes as an automatic system of poetic consciousness, Lacan relates both of these concepts to the way societies are structured through the manipulation of symbolic oppositions.[5]

In his seminar, this combination of three different forms of symbolism (primary, social, and subjective) is soon displaced by the focus on how in each of these systems, individuals are included by being excluded.[6] Lacan, thus, represents the subject of the unconscious as a lack, a gap, and a fault in order to stress the negative presence of this entity: “For what the unconscious does is to show us the gap through which neurosis recreates a harmony with a real--a real that may well not be determined. In this gap, something happens" (22). Instead of basing the unconscious on repression, Lacan concentrates on the way the subject is included in symbolization by being excluded.

This definition of the unconscious can be related to the fact that people within a social system are not aware of the rules and practices shaping that culture. For instance, Levi-Strauss found that the members of "primitive" groups strictly followed rules that they could not explain as they took all symbolic social formations to be natural and real.[7] Freud makes a similar claim in *Totem and Taboo*, but Freud's main point was that these animistic subjects projected their own thoughts onto the external world as they were dominated by the primary processes.[8] Freud added that since they treated words like things and things like words, they confused symbolic memories with perceptions of the real.[9] Following Lacan, we can say that these subjects are excluded from their own thoughts since their internal representations lack intentionality.

Lacan himself will later posit that in the structure of a hallucination, the subject is barred and subverted: "If I have insisted on it, it is to show you that the notion of hallucination, in Freud, as a process of regressive investment on perception necessarily implies that the subject must be completely subverted in it--which he is, in effect, only in extremely fleeting moments" (48). On the level of the primary processes, what we find is that the loss of intentional control (the barring of the subject) is coupled with a projection of thought onto reality, which Lacan reads as proof that the cause of the unconscious is language itself: "But the fact that there is a mode in which Freud can conceive as possible the subversion of the subject shows clearly enough to what extent he identifies the subject with that which is originally subverted by the system of the signifier. So let us leave this time of the unconscious" (48). Instead of following Freud by equating consciousness with the automatic psychotic primary processes, Lacan conflates the unconscious with the primary processes. This displacement has important clinical implications since as Lacan himself insists, the main way to differentiate psychosis from neurosis is by opposing two different defense mechanisms: psychotic foreclosure and neurotic repression.[10]

Lacan's notion of foreclosure is equivalent to Freud's concept of projection in the primary processes because Lacan posits that what is rejected (foreclosed) in the symbolic returns in the real.[11] For example, Freud argued that when paranoid psychotics think that other people know their thoughts, what the psychotic is doing is projecting their own internal self-observations out into the external world.[12] Due to the foreclosure of the super-ego, the psychotic experiences internal thoughts as externalized voices. The idea here is that when people radically reject their own thoughts and feelings, these internal mental representations are experienced as real perceptions coming from the outside.[13] Freud added that this psychotic process represents both the primary state of culture (animism) and the initial state of infantile subjectivity (the hallucination of the satisfaction of desire).[14] Moreover, we gain access to this type of thinking when we dream since the ego of intentionality and reality testing is put to sleep as we hallucinate the representation of our desires, fears, and anxieties.[15]

In contrast to psychotic projection, with neurotic repression, the subject replaces unwanted thoughts, perceptions, and feelings with imaginary fantasies leading to the formation of symptoms and the generation of defensive counter-measures.[16] While in psychosis, thoughts and feelings are rejected and then perceived as coming from the other in the real, in neurosis, unwanted feelings and thoughts are repressed and return in a distorted form. This distinction is crucial from the perspective of treatment because psychotics should not be put on a couch and asked to free associate since they will quickly regress to the primary processes.[17] Here we see how the theoretical distinction between the unconscious and the primary processes is so essential; if we do not understand this difference, we could make a major clinical mistake.

The Dream of the Subject

Freud's theory of the primary processes is so vital to not only our understanding of psychosis but also to our work with neurotics because this system shapes dreams and other neurotic formations. In fact, Freud insists that dreams are a psychosis of short duration, and they are the best way to encounter unconscious material.[18] According to his theory, once a neurotic subject avoids unwanted thoughts, feelings, and memories, these mental experiences become reshaped by the primary processes of association, substitution, and displacement. Lacan adds that in the neurotic's dream state, the subjectivity of the unconscious is evident in the way that each representation is coupled with a subjective response:

> If you keep hold of this initial structure, you will avoid giving yourself up to some partial aspect of the question of the unconscious---as, for example, that it is the subject, qua alienated in his history, at the level at which the syncope of discourse is joined with his desire. You will see that, more radically, it is in the dimension of a synchrony that you must situate the unconscious--at the level of a being, but in the sense that it can spread over everything, that is to say, at the level of the subject of the enunciation, in so far as, according to the sentences, according to the modes, it loses itself as much as it finds itself again, and in the sense that, in an interjection, in an imperative, in an invocation, even in a hesitation, it is always the unconscious that presents you with its enigma, and speaks--in short, at the level at which everything that blossoms in the unconscious spreads, like mycelium, as Freud says about the dream, around a central point. It is always a question of the subject qua indeterminate ... (26)

On one level, Lacan is arguing the subjectivity spreads over the entire dream because in relation to representation, the ego is absent and the subject vacillates and is indeterminate; however, on another level, he is insisting that the subject is present through the emotional relation to the symbolic representations. In the opposition between the content of the dream and the subjective response to the content, we find the relation between the primary processes and the unconscious. Like the final punctuation of a sentence with a question mark or an exclamation point, subjectivity (the enunciation in linguistic terminology) defines the meaning of a symbolic representation through the attitude of the speaker or writer in relation to symbolic material.[19] In fact, what one often finds in dreams is an ongoing commentary similar to a voice-over in movies.

The dream then highlights two aspects of the primary processes: the manifest symbols (signifiers) and the latent thoughts (signifieds). As Lacan highlights, Freud anticipates Saussure's theory of linguistics by separating these two different aspects of language; on one level, we find the automatic association of symbolic representations in a network of memories, and on another level, these representations are interpreted through subjective desire.[20] Lacan emphasizes this latter point by claiming that desire and interpretation are the same thing since meaning, feelings, and subjectivity are equated.[21] What then happens in free association is that the network of symbolic associations is explored as the subjective responses to these representations becomes evident. However, it would be wrong to equate the recounting of the dream with the dream itself since they are presented in radically different ways.

In following Descartes' discussion of thought as the essence of consciousness, Lacan interjects his theory of the subject into his definition of the unconscious:

> To all these forms of unconscious, ever more or less linked to some obscure will regarded as primordial, to something preconscious, what Freud opposes is the revelation that at the level of the unconscious there is something at all points homologous with what occurs at the level of the subject--this thing speaks and functions in a way quite as elaborate as at the level of the conscious, which thus loses what seemed to be its privilege. I am well aware of the resistances that this simple remark can still provoke, though it is evident in everything that Freud wrote. (24)

The radical move Lacan makes here is to define consciousness and subjectivity through the psychotic dream state. Since we are not in control of our dreams, and they do not follow our intentions, we are subjected to them, and yet, our subjectivity is evident in these formations. Here, Lacan is close to Sartre's critique of Freud since one of Sartre's main criticisms of psychoanalysis was that it tried to divorce subjectivity from consciousness through the concept of the unconscious.[22] For Sartre, even when we try to repress something or avoid a memory, we are conscious of what we are doing. However, what Sartre refuses to accept is the difference between consciousness in the primary processes and the way repression causes a division between the unintentional awareness of consciousness and the lack of awareness of repressed material.[23] Although Lacan helps to reject Sartre's criticism by showing how consciousness itself combines automatic symbolism with projection and interpretation, what he does not consistently articulate is the distinction between the primary processes and repression.

As I have been arguing, a major point of confusion in Lacan's text is the relationship between foreclosure (projection) in the primary processes and repression as the cause of the unconscious. This issue comes out in his discussion of censorship:

> Oblivium is that which effaces-effaces what? The signifier as such. Here we find again the basic structure that makes it possible, in an operatory way, for something to take on the function of barring, striking out another thing. This is a more primordial level, structurally speaking, than repression, of which we shall speak later. Well, this operatory element of effacement is what Freud designates, from the outset, in the function of the censor. (26–27)

It should be clear that Lacan wants to distinguish a primary level of censorship from a secondary level of repression, but what confuses matters is that both of these defenses rely on striking out a signifier. What needs to be distinguished is that with the primary processes, it is the intentional ego that is absent, while with neurosis, a signifier has been barred from consciousness.

Lacan clarifies this distinction by turning to Freud's example of forgetting a name because part of the signifier reminds Freud of things he would like to not admit to himself:[24]

> Let us turn again to an example that has never been sufficiently exploited, the first used by Freud to demonstrate his theory, namely, his forgetting, his inability to remember the word Signorelli after his visit to the paintings at Orvieto. Is it possible not to see emerging from the text itself, and establishing itself, not metaphor, but the reality of the disappearance, of the suppression, of the Unterdrückung, the passing underneath? The term Signor, Herr, passes underneath--the absolute master, I once said, which is in fact death, has disappeared there. Furthermore, do we not see, behind this, the emergence of that which forced Freud to find in the myths of the death of the father the regulation of his desire? After all, it is to be found in Nietzsche, who declares, in his own myth, that God is dead. And it is

> perhaps against the background of the same reasons. For the myth of the God is dead--which, personally, I feel much less sure about, as a myth of course, than most contemporary intellectuals, which is in no sense a declaration of theism, nor of faith in the resurrection--perhaps this myth is simply a shelter against the threat of castration. (27)

There is a lot going on in this passage, but what I would like to stress is Lacan's emphasis on the notion that Freud cannot remember a name because part of the signifier reminds him of death and castration. Clearly, we are on the level of repression and the unconscious here what determines the self-censorship is the desire to avoid thinking about a threatening subject matter.[25] Lacan adds that we know in analysis when we are dealing with the unconscious because the subject is surprised by what is discovered in his or her own discourse: "Thus the unconscious is always manifested as that which vacillates in a split in the subject, from which emerges a discovery that Freud compares with desire--a desire that we will temporarily situate in the denuded metonymy of the discourse in question, where the subject surprises himself in some unexpected way" (28). While the subject of a psychotic hallucination or delusion is certain about what is being perceived, the subject of the unconscious is surprised by the automatic return of the repressed.[26] It is then a goal of analysis to enable an encounter with this unexpected material.

Underlying both Freud's and Lacan's conceptions of the unconscious is the notion that whatever is repressed always tries to return.[27] In fact, Lacan uses his theory of desire to show how in contrast to the pleasure principle, unconscious material resists being subjected to the homeostatic drive to avoid all tension and conflict: "Pleasure limits the scope of human possibility--the pleasure principle is a principle of homeostasis. Desire, on the other hand, finds its boundary, its strict relation, its limit, and it is in the relation to this limit that it is sustained as such, crossing the threshold imposed by the pleasure principle" (31). From this perspective, what allows us to move beyond the dictates of the pleasure principle is desire as a longing for something we do not have that also refuses to be limited by time or the need to avoid tension:[28]

> Now, although desire merely conveys what it maintains of an image of the past towards an ever short and limited future, Freud declares that it is nevertheless indestructible. Notice that in the term indestructible, it is precisely the most inconsistent reality of all that is affirmed. If indestructible desire escapes from time, to what register does it belong in the order of things? For what is a thing, if not that which endures, in an identical state, for a certain time? Is not this the place to distinguish in addition to duration, the substance of things, another mode of time--a logical time? (31–32)

This notion that desire is indestructible points to its symbolic character because real things are affected by time, while symbolic representations can resist temporality. In fact, early on in his work, Lacan stressed that our awareness of lack and absence is only possible because we have a symbolic marker for something, and as Sartre insisted, nothing lacks in the real.[29] Desire then is a symbolic representation of something that can be lost or absent, and it is this presence of absence that opens up the human experience to life beyond reality and biology. The symbol, then, not only kills the thing, but it also makes us desire the thing that has been lost.[30]

Repetition and Desire

Lacan's discussion of desire pushes him to introduce the second concept, repetition, which he quickly distinguishes from transference:

> It is quite common, for example, to hear it said that the transference is a form of repetition. I am not saying that this is untrue, or that there is not an element of repetition in the transference. I am not saying that it is not on the basis of his experience of the transference that Freud approached repetition. What I am saying is that the concept of repetition has nothing to do with the concept of the transference. Because of this confusion, I am obliged to go through this explanation at the outset, to lay down the necessary logical steps. For to follow chronology would be to encourage the ambiguities of the concept of repetition that derive from the fact that its discovery took place in the course of the first hesitant steps necessitated by the experience of the transference. (31)

Lacan reveals here how his method of presentation requires both relating and distinguishing key concepts. Moreover, he posits that Freud's theories can be confusing because they were derived from Freud's developing technique. The importance of this latter point is that we see the close connection between theory and practice, which requires us to constantly ask how a particular concept helps to shape psychoanalytic technique.

By focusing on analytic treatment, Lacan recenters our understanding of Freud's theory of the unconscious:

> The status of the unconscious, which, as I have shown, is so fragile on the ontic plane, is ethical. In his thirst for truth, Freud says, whatever it is, I must go there, because, somewhere, this unconscious reveals itself. And he says this on the basis of his experience of what was, up to that time, for the physician, the most rejected, the most concealed, the most contained, reality, that of the hysteric, in so far as it is--in a sense, from its origin--marked by the sign of deception. (33)

Lacan's important move here is to posit that the ethics of psychoanalysis is based on the desire to uncover unconscious material no matter how uncomfortable or difficult the process might be.[31] Furthermore, he adds that this pursuit of the truth required Freud to work with hysterical subjects, who were up to that point avoided by the medical profession because of their deceptive nature. I would add that Freud uses the concept of the reality principle in order to define the ethics of psychoanalysis since for Freud, the unconscious is defined by self-deception, and it is only a process of radical self-honesty that allows the discovery of surprising repressed material through the process of free association enabled by the neutrality of the analyst.[32]

Unlike most other analysts and therapists today, Lacan's discourse is full of reference to truth, the real, and ethics, and one reason for this focus on these issues is that he sees psychoanalytic practice as centered on the repetition of deception and the need to follow speech wherever it leads: "We shall see how by means of repetition, as repetition of deception, Freud coordinates experience, qua deceiving, with a real that will henceforth be situated in the field of science, situated as that which the subject is condemned to miss, but even this miss is revelatory" (39).

Lacan thus approaches the reality principle, science, and the ethics of psychoanalysis through the concept of repetition, which he relates to the revelation caused by a missed encounter with the real.[33]

Lacan connects science and the reality principle to the concept of repetition because he sees this notion as highlighting both the impossibility of fully symbolizing reality and the fact that the real always returns.[34] Since we cannot completely escape our own memories, thoughts, fears, and feelings, psychoanalytic practice is founded on a belief in the power of repetition. In fact, Lacan points to this role of repetition in psychoanalytic technique by making the following argument:

> Where it was, the *Ich*--the subject, not psychology--the subject, must come into existence. And there is only one method of knowing that one is there, namely, to map the network. And how is a network mapped? One goes back and forth over one's ground, one crosses one's path, one cross-checks it always in the same way, and in this seventh chapter of *The Interpretation of Dreams* there is no other confirmation for one's Gewissheit, one's certainty, than this--Speak of chance, gentlemen, if you like. In my experience I have observed nothing arbitrary in this field, for it is crosschecked in such a way that it escapes chance. (45)

In saying that analysis has to map the network of the subject's memories, Lacan is emphasizing how the practice of free association relies on discovering repressed memories by following the path of their associations. From this perspective, there is no chance because all connections have been determined through symbolic relationships that are discovered through repetition. Since, as Freud insists, no memory can ever be fully forgotten, these thoughts and feelings are seen as equivalent to a real that always returns to the same place.[35]

The practice of free association and the neutrality of the analysis are, thus, based on a belief in the return and repetition of signifiers. Since all thoughts and feelings are encoded in memories, and all memories are signifiers, this theory of the inability to efface signifiers represents the key to both the theory and technique of psychoanalysis.[36] Furthermore, Lacan shows that in Freud's work, an important move was made by separating these memory signifiers from consciousness and perception:

> Well, to return to the letter to Fliess, how do the *Wahrnehmungszeichen*, the traces of perception, function? Freud deduces from his experience the need to make an absolute separation between perception and consciousness--in order for these traces of perception to pass into memory, they must first be effaced in perception, and reciprocally. He then designates a time when these Wahrnehmungszeichen must be constituted in simultaneity. What is this time, if not signifying synchrony? And, of course, Freud says this all the more in that he does not know that he is saying it fifty years before the linguists. But we can immediately give to these Wahrnehmungszeichen their true name of signifiers. (45–46)

Lacan's insight here is that Freud anticipates structural linguistics by treating the signs of perception as signifiers located in a synchronic network. One of the effects of this theory of the signifier is that memory is no longer founded on perception or consciousness since each internal mental representation is a signifier relating to other signifiers through the processes of differentiation, association, and substitution. In this system, free association is dedicated to tracing the relations contained in the internal network.[37]

The theory of the signifier, therefore, becomes essential in providing the foundations of analytic practice:

> Recollection is not Platonic reminiscence--it is not the return of a form, an imprint, a eidos of beauty and good, a supreme truth, coming to us from the beyond. It is something that comes to us from the structural necessities, something humble, born at the level of the lowest encounters and of all the talking crowd that precedes us, at the level of the structure of the signifier, of the languages spoken in a stuttering, stumbling way, but which cannot elude constraints whose echoes, model, style can be found, curiously enough, in contemporary mathematics. (47)

By seeing recollection as based on the network of signifiers, Lacan is able to provide a scientific foundation for psychoanalysis. This theory works by eliminating mystical and mythical conceptions of memory through the mathematical mapping of signifying structures.[38]

As I argued in Chap. 2, the *Project for a Scientific Psychology* treated memories, neurons, and thoughts as signifiers defined by their difference to other signifiers, and in this anticipation of structural linguistics, Freud cleared a space for his conceptions of repetition and free association: "As you saw with the notion of cross-checking, the function of return, *Wiederkehr*, is essential. It is not only *Wiederkehr* in the sense of that which has been repressed--the very constitution of the field of the unconscious is based on the Wiederkehr. It is there that Freud bases his certainty" (47–48). The certainty of the analyst is produced by the trust that one has in the theory of the return of repressed signifiers, which structures free association and the discovery of unconscious material.[39]

By making repetition, and not the reality principle, a fundamental concept, Lacan seeks to separate the testing of reality from the subject's ego or an identification with the analyst's sense of reality. Lacan also uses his conception of the real to highlight how there is always a difference between reality and how we represent it:

> *Wiederholen* is related to *Erinnerung* (remembering). The subject in himself, the recalling of his biography, all this goes only to a certain limit, which is known as the real.... An adequate thought, qua thought, at the level at which we are, always avoids--if only to find itself again later in everything the same thing. Here, the real is that which always comes back to the same place--to the place where the subject in so far as he thinks, where the res cogitans, does not meet it. (49)

Just as Freud argued that there is a center to every dream that has no meaning, Lacan insists that since the symbolic cannot fully represent the real, every attempt at memory ultimately fails.[40] In fact, for Freud, what defined science was the acceptance of the limits of our knowledge, which fuels a desire to always try to discover more. Furthermore, Freud sought to counter what he calls the "omnipotence of thought" in the primary processes by stressing the limitations of our understanding.[41]

Lacan's theory of the real can be seen as representing Freud's reality principle because what he seeks to emphasize is the fact that reality always resists representation: "Where do we meet this real? For what we have in the discovery of psycho-analysis is an encounter, an essential encounter--an appointment to which we are always called with a real that eludes us" (53). Based on this theory of the real as always being missed, we see how free association involves two opposite movements: one aspect concerns re-tracing the network of the memory associations, and the other aspect concerns accepting the limitations of speech and memory: "The real is beyond the automaton, the return, the coming-back, the insistence of the signs, by which we see ourselves governed by the pleasure principle. The real is that which always lies behind the automaton, and it is quite obvious, throughout Freud's research, that it is this that is the object of his concern" (54). From this perspective, we can say that there are two reals in psychoanalysis: the reality of the internal system of signifiers and the reality of the fundamental conflict between the symbolic and the real.[42]

One reason why this conflict between the symbolic and the real is so important to life and the experience of psychoanalysis is that Lacan defines trauma by the missed symbolic encounter with the real: "The function of the *tuche*, of the real as encounter--the encounter in so far as it may be missed, in so far as it is essentially the missed encounter--first presented itself in the history of psycho-analysis in a form that was in itself already enough to arouse our attention, that of the trauma" (55). Since the real by definition is impossible to symbolize, but it always returns to the same place, it represents a traumatic encounter.[43]

Ultimately, for Lacan, the real is represented as traumatic because it undermines the pleasure principle's drive to avoid all tension and conflict:

> In effect, the trauma is conceived as having necessarily been marked by the subjectifying homeostasis that orientates the whole functioning defined by the pleasure principle. Our experience then presents us with a problem, which derives from the fact that, at the very heart of the primary processes, we see preserved the insistence of the trauma in making us aware of its existence. The trauma reappears, in effect, frequently unveiled. How can the dream, the bearer of the subject's desire, produce that which makes the trauma emerge repeatedly--if not its very face, at least the screen that shows us that it is still there behind? (55)

Lacan asks here how it is possible for people to return in their minds to traumatic events if our thinking is driven by the pleasure principle's quest to avoid all mental tension and unpleasure? In other words, why do we repeat in our dreams and fantasies the very things we are trying to escape?[44]

Lacan's strange response to these questions is the following: "Let us conclude that the reality system, however far it is developed, leaves an essential part of what belongs to the real a prisoner in the toils of the pleasure principle" (55). Lacan appears to be arguing here that the reason why we repeat traumatic events in our minds and actions is that the pleasure principle maintains control over part of the real. However, if we return to Freud's fundamental concepts, it would be more accurate to state that while the primary processes may first act to satisfy the dictates of the pleasure principle, the automatic nature of these symbolic processes make them prone to return to thoughts and experiences that the subject would like to avoid. In this structure, the repetition of the trauma is caused by the fact that we do not totally control our own minds, and we cannot efface our memory signifiers.[45] What then makes us ethical is that we can never fully avoid our guilt, shame, fear, and truth.

Repression and Consciousness

In order to show what allows us to not think about the reality of our minds, Lacan follows his discussion of traumatic repetition with an examination of how our "normal" consciousness is constituted:

> The other day, I was awoken from a short nap by knocking at my door just before I actually awoke. With this impatient knocking I had already formed a dream, a dream that manifested to me something other than this knocking. And when I awake, it is in so far as I reconstitute my entire representation around this knocking--this perception-that I am aware of it. I know that I am there, at what time I went to sleep, and why I went to sleep. When the knocking occurs, not in my perception, but in my consciousness, it is because my consciousness reconstitutes itself around this representation--that I know that I am waking up, that I am knocked up. (56)

The first thing to highlight about this discussion of self-consciousness is the way that it begins with the automatic symbolization of reality in the dream.[46] Through the primary processes, the knocking on the door is instantly transformed into a scene of something related to that perceived sound. Here we witness the automatic translation of perceptions into imaginary symbolic representations beyond the intentionality and control of the subject. Since Lacan is aware of the manifest content of his dream, we can say that the initial form of consciousness is hallucinatory. What then happens as he awakes is that he convinces himself that he is in control of his mind by locating his self in time and space. In this process, his knowledge becomes identified with his ego as he takes responsibility for his own thoughts and perceptions.[47]

As Freud argues in his *Project*, one of the main ways of distinguishing the consciousness of the dream from the consciousness of the waking state is that in the second form, the ego uses attention, selection, and repression to make thoughts, feelings, and perceptions appear to be the product of the self's intentionality.[48] Lacan's version of this argument is the following: "Observe what I am directing you towards--towards the symmetry of that structure that makes me, after the awakening knock, able to sustain myself, apparently only in a relation with my representation, which, apparently, makes of me only consciousness. A sort of involuted reflection--in my consciousness, it is only my representation that I recover possession of" (57). The consciousness of the ego is here defined by the illusion that "I" control "my" thinking.

Instead of directly stressing the role of repression in the formation of the ego's consciousness, Lacan makes another curious move by introducing his theory of the object (a). In returning to the traumatic encounter with the unrepresentable real, Lacan seeks to take on the history of philosophy by representing the object (a) as the which presents the truth of the real as the inverse of self-consciousness and aesthetic contemplation: "In so far as it is a search for truth, is this way to be forged in our style of adventure, with its trauma seen as a reflection of facticity? Or is it to be located where tradition has always placed it, at the level of the dialectic of truth and appearance, grasped at the outset of perception in its fundamentally ideic, in a way aesthetic, and accentuated character as visual centering? (71). This consideration of visual centering indicates the key role that images and the mapping of space play in Lacan's conception of the ego and narcissism.[49] Following Freud, Lacan highlights how the ego is formed through the identification with a holistic image or spatial mapping, which provides the self with a sense of imaginary bodily and mental unity.[50] Moreover, the sense of intentionality and mental control is derived in part from the formation of the ego as contained in a body separated from others. We shall see that the opposite of this idealized ego control and idealization is the object (a) as an entity that lacks a spectral image.[51]

Turning to the work of the phenomenologist Maurice Merleau-Ponty, Lacan illustrates the conflict between the philosophy of consciousness and the psychoanalytic understanding of the real: "This work, *Le Visible et l'invisible*, may indicate for us the moment of arrival of the philosophical tradition--the tradition that begins with Plato with the promulgation of the idea, of which one may say that, setting out from an aesthetic world, it is determined by an end given to being as sovereign good, thus attaining a beauty that is also its limit. And it is not by chance that Maurice Merleau-Ponty recognized its guide in the eye" (71). The argument here is that philosophy bases consciousness on vision and the perception of ideal moral and aesthetic forms. As Lacan indicates, underlying this vision-centered tradition is Merleau-Ponty's focus on the intentionality of the knowing ego:

> In this work, one finds a recapitulation of the regulatory function of form, invoked in opposition to that which, as philosophical thinking progressed, had been taken to that extreme of vertigo expressed in the term idealism--how could the 'lining' that representation then became be joined to that which it is supposed to cover? *La Phinomenologie* brings us back, then, to the regulation of form, which is governed, not only by the subject's eye, but by his expectations, his movement, his grip, his muscular and visceral emotion--in short, his constitutive presence, directed in what is called his total intentionality. (71)

Unlike the unintentional primary processes shaping consciousness, the ego is centered on the intentionality of the knowing self.[52] What then enables us to move from the barred subject of projection and hallucination to the centered ego is the formation of a point of view guided by expectation.

It is important to point out that while Lacan stresses the visual aspects of this imaginary structure, he also realizes that since blind people can also develop an ego and a holistic body image, the formation of the self must be based on a virtual mapping of space.[53] Our recognition and identification with an ideal body image, then, relies on our ability to identify with an external holistic object. Thus, in his theory of the mirror stage, Lacan highlights how the ideal ego is formed by identifying with the ideal image in the mirror, and this object can be replaced by the relation to another person of similar size and age.[54]

The next move that Lacan makes in relation to this imaginary level of subjectivity is to oppose the intentionality of the ego to his concept of the gaze:

> You will see that the ways through which he will lead you are not only of the order of visual phenomenology, since they set out to rediscover--this is the essential point-the dependence of the visible on that which places us under the eye of the seer. But this is going too far, for that eye is only the metaphor of something that I would prefer to call the seer's 'shoot' (pousse)--something prior to his eye. What we have to circumscribe, by means of the path he indicates for us, is the pre-existence of a gaze--I see only from one point, but in my existence I am looked at from all sides. (72)

Since I see the world from my own perspective, I repress the way I am seen by others. The gaze, then, represents a reversal of my intentionality and a threat to my ego.[55] Just as in a dream, I am shown something to look at, which is not controlled by my expectations, with the gaze, I am looked at from the position of the primary processes.

Lacan ties this theory of the gaze to the production of anxiety in the face of the threat of castration: "The gaze is presented to us only in the form of a strange contingency, symbolic of what we find on the horizon, as the thrust of our experience, namely, the lack that constitutes castration anxiety" (72–73). From this perspective, what causes anxiety is the reversal of our intentionality since we can no longer control what we are experiencing.[56] The ego therefore has to repress the primary processes because these representations are not the products of our intentions: In the dream, the slip of the tongue, and the symptom, we reveal more than we want to reveal because we have lost control of our own minds. Furthermore, free association is predicated on this notion that we need to learn how to speak without intention and control in order to discover the things we would rather repress.

The theory of the ego is thus equivalent to the concept of repression, and this equivalence motivates Lacan to posit that the ego is a primarily a defensive structure, and so it makes no sense to base therapy on trying to strengthen this agency.[57] Once again, we see here how theory matches practice since the possibility of free association is predicated on the critique of ego psychology and the Western philosophical tradition.[58] In turn, the concept of the gaze relates to how our visual and virtual relation to the world and ourselves is always predicated on the repression of the gaze as a representation of the primary processes: "In our relation to things, in so far as this relation is constituted by the way of vision, and ordered in the figures of representation, something slips, passes, is transmitted, from stage to stage, and is always to some degree eluded in it--that is what we call the gaze" (73). The gaze presents here the reversal of our usual form of intentional awareness, and due to its threatening nature, it must always be repressed by the controlling ego.

The cause of repression is thus centered on the ego's need to anticipate what enters consciousness, and this means that the primary processes have to be repressed because they function beyond the ego's control. Lacan's introduction of the gaze as a primary form of what he calls the object (a) is shown here to be guided by the need to explain the relation between repression and the primary processes:

> There is no need for us to refer to some supposition of the existence of a universal seer. If the function of the stain is recognized in its autonomy and identified with that of the gaze, we can seek its track, its thread, its trace, at every stage of the constitution of the world, in the scopic field. We will then realize that the function of the stain and of the gaze is both that which governs the gaze most secretly and that which always escapes from the grasp of that form of vision that is satisfied with itself in imagining itself as consciousness. (74)

The gaze is defined at this point in opposition to the self-satisfaction of the imaginary ego, which relies on visual and spatial control.[59] Since in the dream and the hallucination, we are shown what to look at, we lose the illusion of ego control, and this loss of control is what causes anxiety. For instance, many patients do not want to lie on a coach and free associate because they are afraid of losing control of their own minds. In fact, one reason why it is not a good practice to have psychotic patients lie down and just talk is that they might regress to a pure expression of the primary processes.

In this opposition between the gaze and our usual state of consciousness, we find a central cause for Lacan's theory of the imaginary order:

> Similarly, in that order, which is particularly satisfying for the subject, connoted in psycho-analytic experience by the term narcissism-in which I have striven to reintroduce the essential structure it derives from its reference to the specular image--in the satisfaction, not to say self-satisfaction, that diffuses from it, which gives the subject a pretext for such a profound meconnaissance--and does its empire not extend as far as this reference of the philosophical tradition represented by plenitude encountered by the subject in the mode of contemplation--can we not also grasp that which has been eluded, namely, the function of the gaze? (74)

Although Freud introduces his theory of how the ego is formed by developing his concept of narcissism, he never fully explores the role played by the mapping of space in the production of the ideal ego.[60] What Lacan does by turning to the field of philosophy is to show the limits of the intentionality of consciousness. Instead of privileging the contemplative ego of visual and cognitive control, Lacan sees the ego as based on a set of misrecognitions that can be reversed by the presence of the gaze.

As stated above, the concept of the gaze helps us to comprehend the conflict between the primary processes and the desire for ego control: "What does this mean, if not that, in the so-called waking state, there is an elision of the gaze, and an elision of the fact that not only does it look, it also shows. In the field of the dream, on the other hand, what characterizes the images is that it shows" (74). One has to only think about the experience of dreaming to realize that on the level of the primary processes, we are not in control of what we are perceiving or thinking. The gaze is a threat to our narcissism and our drive to see only what we want to see and to think only what we want to think, and the practice of psychoanalysis requires a reversal of this narcissism.[61]

In connecting Lacan's theory to the practice of psychoanalysis, I am not only clarifying the key concepts of the field, but I am also resisting the academic temptation to simply apply his ideas without any connection to the fundamental system and experience from which they are derived. For instance, in film theory, the gaze has often been used to represent the control of narrative and culture through the masculine direction of visual representation. However, as we have seen, the gaze presents the opposite of control:[62]

> It shows--but here, too, some form of 'sliding away' of the subject is apparent. Look up some description of a dream, any one--not only the one I referred to last time, in which, after all, what I am going to say may remain enigmatic, but any dream--place it in its co-ordinates, and you will see that this it shows is well to the fore. So much is it to the fore, with the characteristics in which it is co-ordinated-namely, the absence of horizon, the enclosure, of that which is contemplated in the waking state, and, also, the character of emergence, of contrast, of stain, of its images, the intensification of their colours--that, in the final resort, our position in the dream is profoundly that of someone who does not see. The subject does not see where it is leading, he follows. He may even on occasion detach himself, tell himself that it is a dream, but in no case will he be able to apprehend himself in the dream in the way in which, in the Cartesian cogito, he apprehends himself as thought. (75)

Instead of us looking at the dream, we are shown what to see, and this reversal of intentionality gives us access to unconscious material that has been transformed by the primary processes. Lacan adds that what Descartes got wrong in his famous "I think, therefore, I am" is the fact that in the dream, the ego slips away. In fact, this effacement of the "I" is similar to the Eastern meditative notion that the self is an illusion.[63]

In mediation, the dream state, and the hallucination, the primary processes think without an ego, as one is forced to see what one may prefer to repress: "In a dream, he is a butterfly. What does this mean? It means that he sees the butterfly in his reality as gaze. What are so many figures, so many shapes, so many colours, if not this gratuitous showing, in which is marked for us the primal nature of the essence of the gaze" (76). The dream here presents the reversal of our normal consciousness through the lack of ego intentionality and the presence of the gaze. From a clinical perspective, this theory of reversal is so important because it helps to explain why we need free association to move beyond repression in order to access unconscious material.

Transference

Following his articulation of the gaze and the reversal of intentionality, Lacan introduces the concept of transference: "This brings us to the function of the transference. For this indeterminate of pure being that has no point of access to determination, this primary position of the unconscious that is articulated as constituted by the indetermination of the subject--it is to this that the transference gives us access, in an enigmatic way. It is a Gordian knot that leads us to the following conclusion--the subject is looking for his certainty" (129). Lacan posits here that since the subject of the primary processes lacks intentionality and a determinant status, the patient seeks certainty through transference. In other words, just as Descartes has to return to the idea of a perfect and all-knowing god in order to escape from his own feelings of radical doubt, the patient in analysis idealizes the analyst in order to find a person who knows and is certain.[64]

Following Freud, Lacan stresses that in transference, the subject hands over responsibility over to the Other:

> One may go so far as to believe that the opacity of the trauma--as it was then maintained in its initial function by Freud's thought, that is to say, in my terms, its resistance to signification--is then specifically held responsible for the limits of remembering. And, after all, it is hardly surprising, given my own theorization, that I should see this as a highly significant moment in the transfer of powers from the subject to the Other, what I call the capital Other (le grand Autre), the locus of speech and, potentially, the locus of truth. (129)

Since the traumatic real resists symbolization, and the gaze of the primary processes reverses intentional control, the patient in analysis seeks to find some certainty by seeing the analyst as the One who knows The Truth. In fact, Freud argued that when a patient suddenly stopped free associating, he was sure that the subject was thinking about the presence of the analyst.[65]

Lacan insists that we should see the transference as a necessary obstacle to free association and the discovery of unconscious material: "The transference is the means by which the communication of the unconscious is interrupted, by which the unconscious closes up again. Far from being the handing over of powers to the unconscious, the transference is, on the contrary, its closing up" (130). Repressed material and the formations of the primary processes are thus avoided through the transference, but this avoidance has to be worked through.[66] However, what Lacan finds in many forms of therapy and analysis is a reinforcing of the transference, which is caused by a misunderstanding of its essential structure:

> There is a conception which, wherever it is formulated, can only contaminate practice--I am referring to the conception which would have the analysis of the transference proceed on the basis of an alliance with the healthy part of the subject's ego, and consists in appealing to his common sense, by way of pointing out to him the illusory character of certain of his actions in his relation with the analyst. This is a thesis that subverts what it is all about, namely the bringing to awareness of this split in the subject, realized here, in fact, in presence. To appeal to some healthy part of the subject thought to be there in the real, capable of judging with the analyst what is happening in the transference, is to misunderstand that it is precisely this part that is concerned in the transference, that it is this part that closes the door, or the window, or the shutters, or whatever--and that the beauty with whom one wishes to speak is there, behind, only too willing to open the shutters again. That is why it is at this moment that interpretation becomes decisive, for it is to the beauty one must speak. (130–131)

From Lacan's perspective, the analyst's interpretation should be aimed at enabling the discovery of unconscious material, but what has to be avoided is feeding the illusion that the analyst is the one who knows the truth of reality.[67] While many other analysts and therapist seek to form an alliance between the "healthy" parts of the patient's ego and the analyst's reality testing, Lacan sees this relationship as only sustaining a defensive illusion.[68]

As Freud in his *Project* bases transference on the initial dependence of the helpless child on the caregiver, Lacan emphasizes the relation between love and deception:

> When I introduced you to the subject of Cartesian certainty as the necessary starting-point of all our speculations as to what the unconscious reveals, I pointed out the role of essential balancer played in Descartes by the Other which, it is said, must on no account be deceptive. In analysis, the danger is that this Other will be deceived. This is not the only dimension to be apprehended in the transference. But one has to admit that if there is one domain in which, in discourse, deception has some chance of success, it is certainly love that provides its model. What better way of assuring oneself, on the point on which one is mistaken, than to persuade the other of the truth of what one says! Is not this a fundamental structure of the dimension of love that the transference gives us the opportunity of depicting? In persuading the other that he has that which may complement us, we assure ourselves of being able to continue to misunderstand precisely what we lack. (133)

Lacan's main point here is that the transference is structured by two demands: one demand is for the analyst to be a source of truth, and the other demand is for the analyst to be the missing thing that will complete the subject.[69] In seeing both of these demands as being based on deception, Lacan returns to Freud's theory of love, hypnosis, and group formations since the foundation of the primal social link is founded on the helpless child's demand for love, recognition, and understanding, which requires the deceptive idealization of the Other.[70]

Lacan affirms that because most therapists and analysts do not understand the deceptive and idealizing nature of transference, they try to get their patients to conform to an illusionary mode of pleasure: "He then seeks for assurances in theories that operate in the direction of an orthopaedic, conformist therapeutics, providing access for the subject to the most mythical conception of happiness [English in the original-Tr.]. Together with an uncritical manipulation of evolutionism, this is what sets the tone of our era" (135). Through this combination of social conformity and evolutionary theory, analysts and therapists seek to motivate their patients to assimilate to a cultural ideal of pleasure. In fact, Lacan argues that the first generation of analysts leaving Europe to set up shop in America wanted their patients to follow the same path of assimilating to American culture that they had to follow.[71] From this perspective, if the analyst feeds the transference relationship, the patient will be pushed to conform to the social ideals of the analyst.

One of Lacan's important moves is to tie the idealizing transference to the narcissistic relationship between the ideal ego and the ego ideal: "it is in the Other that the subject is constituted as ideal, that he has to regulate the completion of what comes as ego, or ideal ego--which is not the ego ideal--that is to say, to constitute himself in his imaginary reality" (144). The idealization of the analyst is thus driven by a desire to idealize the self since the ego ideal is the place in the Other that subject sees himself as loveable.[72] For instance, in his theory of the mirror stage, Lacan pointed out how after a child becomes happy by seeing its own completed image in the mirror, it turns to the caregiver to get a look of approval.[73] The Other, as caregiver, stands here for the social order of cultural ideals, and so what the subject is looking for is not only the verification of the ideal ego but also a recognition of his or her conformity to cultural ideals.[74]

Lacan adds that the ego ideal is the place from which the subject looks at himself and is also the place from which he speaks: "it is in the space of the Other that he sees himself and the point from which he looks at himself is also in that space. Now, this is also the point from which he speaks ... "(144). Lacan posits that that we see ourselves from the position of cultural ideals internalized in the form of the ego ideal; moreover, our speech is also derived from this idealized cultural Other. This theory of transference can be considered to be a restating of Freud's argument from his *Project,* where he affirms that the parent's response to the helpless child's cry represents the origins of human communication and morality.

In this structure, transference presents the fundamental way that we become social subjects, and it is precisely this mode of alienating conformity that has to be exposed through analysis: "the transference is not the enactment (*mise en acte*) of the illusion that seems to drive us to this alienating identification that any conformity constitutes, even when it is with an ideal model, of which the analyst, in any case, cannot be the support--the transference is the enactment of the reality of the unconscious" (146). In contrast to the theory that the patient should identify with the ideals of the analyst as a way of conforming to the expectations of society, Lacan insists that the transference should be used to enable an encounter with the reality of repressed material.

The Unconscious and Sexuality

Following Freud, Lacan posits that the reality of the unconscious is shaped by sexuality, but sexuality is itself defined by the ways societies symbolize and structure natural differences:

> Existence, thanks to sexual division, rests upon copulation, accentuated in two poles that time--honoured tradition has tried to characterize as the male pole and the female pole. This is because the mainspring of reproduction is to be found there. Around this fundamental reality, there have always been grouped, harmonized, other characteristics, more or less bound up with the finality of reproduction. I can do no more than point out here, what, in the biological register, is associated with sexual differentiation, in the form of secondary sexual characteristics and functions. We know today how, in society, a whole distribution of functions in a play of alternation is grounded on this terrain. It is modern structuralism that has brought this out best, by showing that it is at the level of matrimonial alliance, as opposed to natural generation, to biological lineal descent--at the level therefore of the signifier--that the fundamental exchanges take place and it is there that we find once again that the most elementary structures of social functioning are inscribed in the terms of a combinatory. (150)

One of the essential ideas behind this description of sexuality is the dialectical relationship between biology and culture.[75] Instead of simply denying the importance of nature or rejecting social mediation, Lacan centers his theory of sexuality on the combination of nature and culture.[76] In other words, societies use biological sexual differences in order to structure social relationships through a system of oppositions contained in a combinatory system.[77] The signifier plays an important role because it allows for the translation of natural distinctions into cultural oppositions. Furthermore, it is through guilt, shame, and fear that the drives are subjected to the social order.[78]

The reality of the unconscious is therefore sexual because we repress the conflict between nature and culture. Thus, the argument here is not that the primary processes are by definition sexual or that the drives are purely social; instead, it is the unconscious that is defined by repressed sexuality.[79] Therefore, in contrast to Jung, Lacan rejects the "primitive" way of using sex to structure society: "Now, Jungianism--in so far as it makes of the primitive modes of articulating the world something that survives, the kernel, he says, of the psyche itself--is necessarily accompanied by a repudiation of the term libido, by the neutralization of this function by recourse to a notion of psychical energy, a much more generalized notion of interest" (153). While for Jung, our primary processes are defined by the internalization of primitive cultural oppositions, Lacan highlights the Freudian notion of desire:

> For what Freud intends to make present in the function of this libido is not some archaic relation, some primitive mode of access of thoughts, some world that is there like some shade of an ancient world surviving in ours. The libido is the effective presence, as such, of desire. It is what now remains to indicate desire--which is not substance, but which is there at the level of the primary process, and which governs the very mode of our approach. (153)

Desire is here predicated on the automatic symbolism of the primary processes in relation to the essential conflict between social norms and regulations on the one hand and the drives of the individual on the other hand.[80]

As a reminder of the fundamental conflict between nature and culture, desire can be seen as that which results from the difference between what we need and what we demand:

> I maintain that it is at the level of analysis--if we can take a few more steps forward--that the nodal point by which the pulsation of the unconscious is linked to sexual reality must be revealed. This nodal point is called desire, and the theoretical elaboration that I have pursued in recent years will show you, through each stage of clinical experience, how desire is situated

> in dependence on demand--which, by being articulated in signifiers, leaves a metonymic remainder that runs under it, an element that is not indeterminate, which is a condition both, absolute and unapprehensible, an element necessarily lacking, unsatisfied, impossible, misconstrued (meconnu), an element that is called desire. (154)

What Lacan is describing here is that on the most basic level, when the child asks the caregiver for help, the child is driven by an unconscious desire for love, knowledge, and recognition, and this desire brings the reality of unconscious desire into the transference: "it means that in the transference we must see established the weight of sexual reality. Largely unknown and, up to a point, masked, it runs beneath what happens at the level of the analytic discourse, which is well and truly, as it takes form, that of demand--it is not for nothing that all experience leads us to throw it on to the side of the terms frustration and gratification" (155). Here we see how Lacan's theories have direct implications for the practice of psychoanalysis: the reason why the analyst does not satisfy the demands of the patient is that these demands cannot be fully satiated because they are supported by an underlying impossible desire for complete love, knowledge, and recognition.[81] By not fulfilling the demands of the patient, the analyst is able to allow these desires to surface for the first time.

The Drives and the Pleasure Principle

Lacan's discussion of sexuality and desire in the unconscious leads him to articulate the final concept of the drive, which he is quick to distinguish from biology and evolution: "The constancy of the thrust forbids any assimilation of the drive to a biological function, which always has a rhythm. The first thing Freud says about the drive is, if I may put it this way, that it has no day or night, no spring or autumn, no rise and fall. It is a constant force" (165). The compulsive aspect of our drives therefore reveals a non-biological influence to human sexuality.[82] In fact, Lacan adds that he sees drives and satisfaction as two opposed forces: "Between these two terms--drive and satisfaction--there is set up an extreme antinomy that reminds us that the use of the function of the drive has for me no other purpose than to put in question what is meant by satisfaction" (166). As he will later highlight, even subjects' symptoms give them satisfaction, and yet they are still unhappy, which causes them to seek help:

> It is clear that those with whom we deal, the patients, are not satisfied, as one says, with what they are. And yet, we know that everything they are, everything they experience, even their symptoms, involves satisfaction. They satisfy something that no doubt runs counter to that with which they might be satisfied, or rather, perhaps, they give satisfaction to something. They are not content with their state, but all the same, being in a state that gives so little content, they are content. The whole question boils down to the following--what is contented here? (166)

If the pleasure principle means that we find satisfaction in escaping tension and reality, the question remains why we are not content with our own pleasure?

Lacan's response to this conflict between the drives and the pleasure principle is the following: "I would say that to which they give satisfaction by the ways of displeasure is nevertheless--and this is commonly accepted--the law of pleasure. Let us say that, for this sort of satisfaction, they give themselves too much trouble. Up to a point, it is this too much trouble that is the sole justification of our intervention" (166). Lacan's argument here helps us to think about the clinical implications of working with addicts and perverts since in both of these cases, the subject appears to be driven by the satisfaction of their impulses.[83] While many analysts argue that you cannot analyze a pervert, what Lacan shows us is that the drive is never fully satisfied, and so the object of desire is ultimately lost and impossible.[84] What then makes an addiction compulsive is the lack of satiation: "it is precisely because no object of any *Not*, need, can satisfy the drive. Even when you stuff the mouth--the mouth that opens in the register of the drive--it is not the food that satisfies it, it is, as one says, the pleasure of the mouth. That is why, in analytic experience, the oral drive is encountered at the final term, in a situation in which it does no more than order the menu" (167). Lacan returns here to the relation between desire, demand, and need; since our demands will never satisfy our needs, the satisfaction of our desire remains impossible.[85]

One reason why our drives are always partial and limited is that their fundamental aim is defined by auto-erotism: "If the drive may be satisfied without attaining what, from the point of view of a biological totalization of function, would be the satisfaction of its end of reproduction, it is because it is a partial drive, and its aim is simply this return into circuit ... This theory is present in Freud. He tells us somewhere that the ideal model for auto-eroticism would be a single mouth kissing itself ... (179). In basing the sex drive on self-satisfaction, Freud reveals the self-reflexive feedback loop inherent to our drives, which represents a break with biology and evolution.[86]

The compulsive circuit of auto-erotism is coupled with the fact that any object can become a cause of human desire, and yet we become fixated on particular objects.[87] Lacan adds that the only thing that pushes us to move from an oral object to an anal or phallic object is the intervention of an outside social force: "The passage from the oral drive to the anal drive can be produced not by a process of maturation, but by the intervention of something that does not belong to the field of the drive--by the intervention, the overthrow, of the demand of the Other" (180). What Lacan is showing here is how human sexuality is so different from other animals since the object of our desire is arbitrary and the cause of our development is social. The fundamental concept of the drive therefore represents a major challenge for neuroscience, pharmacology, and evolutionary psychology since human behavior is shown to be motivated by impulses and demands going against the laws of nature and evolution.[88]

From Lacan's perspective, unlike instincts, drives break with the evolutionary goals of reproduction and self-preservation: "The dialectic of the drive is profoundly different both from that which belongs to the order of love and from that which belongs to the well-being of the subject" (206). In contrast to both narcissistic love and the pursuit of individual survival, drives represent a compulsive demand for an impossible satisfaction. We see this structure most clearly with addictions where the pursuit of pleasure can result in self-destruction.[89]

From a clinical perspective, it is important to understand how Freud's diagnostic category of perversion has been mostly replaced by the borderline personality disorder.[90] One reason for this substitution is that the post-Freudian standard diagnostic manual (DSM) seeks to eliminate psychoanalysis in order to focus on a more scientific and biological model. However, if we understand that perverse subjects are dominated by their drives, then we see that the lack of impulse control and the dominance of destructive addictive behaviors in what is now called borderline personalities reveals the non-biological aspects of human desire.[91] Guided by the pleasure principle's goal of avoiding all tension and unpleasure, perverse borderline drives seek to produce and then eliminate stimulation. As in the structure of an orgasm, the aim of the desire is to enter a state of non-desire.[92] Even if we see this law of inertia as a biological principle, it is a biology that goes against evolution.

Working Through Transference and the Drives at the End of Analysis

Since drives are determined by desires that can never be fully satisfied, the non-response of the analyst to the patient's demands allows these fundamental desires to emerge. For Lacan, coupled with this revelation of desire, we find the overcoming of transference and narcissism at the end of analysis:

> It would be odd all the same if this subject who is supposed to know, supposed to know something about you, and who, in fact, knows nothing, should be regarded as liquidated, at the very moment when, at the end of the analysis, he begins at last, about you at least, to know something. It is therefore at the moment what he takes on most substance, that the subject who is supposed to know ought to be supposed to have been vaporized. It can only be a question, then, if the term liquidation has any meaning, of the permanent liquidation of that deception by which the transference tends to be exercised in the direction of the closing up of the unconscious. I have already explained to you how it works, by referring to it the narcissistic relation by which the subject becomes an object worthy of love. From his reference to him who must love, him, he tries to induce the Other into a mirage relation in which he convinces him of being worthy of love. (267)

Since transference is based on the fundamental desire for love, recognition, and understanding, the liquidation of the transference entails a new relation to others.[93] What has to be overcome is the idealization of the Other as the place of knowledge and care. Lacan highlights how this idealization is driven by the narcissistic desire of the patient to feel worthy of love, and in this structure, imaginary love functions to block access to unconscious material.[94]

In turning to Freud's theory of identification in his *Group Psychology and the Analysis of the Ego*, Lacan emphasizes how transference love relies on the relation between the ego ideal and the ideal ego: "The point of the ego ideal is that from which the subject will see himself, as one says, as others see him--which will enable him to support himself in a dual situation that is satisfactory for him from the point of view of love" (268). Love here is posited as a form of alienation and social conformity because it is based on the subject identifying with how others see him or her from the perspective of particular cultural ideals.[95] As we see in narcissistic personality disorders and obsessive-compulsive neurosis, the patient perceives the self as an other for the Other.[96] This doubled alienation is derived from the underlying desire for love, recognition, and care. However, in trying to get the Other to recognize the subject, the subject has to represent the self through the Other's ideals.[97]

By equating transference with deception and narcissism, Lacan reveals how society gets us to see ourselves from the perspective of cultural ideals, norms, and morality: "As a specular mirage, love is essentially deception. It is situated in the field established at the level of the pleasure reference, of that sole signifier necessary to introduce a perspective centered on the Ideal point, capital I, placed somewhere in the Other, from which the Other sees me, in the form I like to be seen" (268). The paradox here is that I would like to be seen by the Other, but in order to accomplish this task, I have to see myself through the eyes of this social representative.[98]

In order to break this narcissistic deadlock, the analyst has to find a way to maintain a distance between the analyst's presence and the patient's demand for identification: "There is a beyond to this identification, and this beyond is defined by the relation and the distance of the objet petit a to the idealizing capital I of identification" (271–272). Lacan's main point here is that the analyst has to refuse being the ego ideal of his patient by resisting the temptation to be the One who knows and cares.[99]

Lacan highlights that the development of Freud's analytic technique is in part inspired by Freud's understanding of his original practice of hypnosis, and that by the time of his *Group Psychology and the Analysis of the Ego,* Freud drew a connection between hypnosis and what Lacan calls "collective fascination" (272). In arguing that in hypnosis, passionate love relations, and social groups, we find the same uncritical submission to an idealized Other, Freud offers not only a critique of therapy but also an analysis of fascism: "Things are such that the only view of the schema that Freud gives of hypnosis, gives by the same token the formula of collective fascination, which was an increasing reality at the time when he wrote that article" (272). Since Freud was writing this text before the start of World War II, we see how his understanding of transference relates to both clinical treatment and social organization.[100] The key then to both the political group and the analytic relation is the combination of the ego ideal with the gaze of the Other: "Freud gives its status to hypnosis by superposing at the same place the objet a as such and this signifying mapping that is called the ego ideal' (272). Since the ego ideal is the social place that determines how I see myself as loveable, when this ideal is attached to the gaze, as the transcending perspective of the primary processes, the subject is forced to suspend all reality testing and submit to the all-powerful leader or lover.[101]

At the end of his seminar, we begin to see why Lacan introduced the concept of the gaze as one of the main forms of what he calls the object (a). As the cause of the reversal of ego intentionality, the gaze disempowers the self, which opens the subject up to social submission:

> adding that the objet a may be identical with the gaze. Well, Freud precisely indicates the nodal point of hypnosis when he formulates that the object is certainly an element that is difficult to grasp in it, but an incontestable one, namely, the gaze of the hypnotizer. Remember what I articulated for you about the function of the gaze, of its fundamental relations to the ink-blot, of the fact that there is already in the world some-

> thing that looks before there is a view for it to see, that the ocellus of animal mimicry is indispensible as a presupposition to the fact that a subject may see and be fascinated, that the fascination of the ink-blot is anterior to the view that discovers it. (272–273)

Lacan's theory of the gaze is therefore developed partially in order to explain how fascination works in love, hypnosis, and social groups.[102] In all of these situations, the imaginary and social identification with cultural ideals is coupled with a loss of control and intentionality. Lacan adds that the end of analysis requires the analyst to reverse the hypnotic relationship by allowing for the fall of idealization and the separation of the gaze from the ego ideal: "It is from this idealization that the analyst has to fall in order to be the support of the separating [object] a, in so far as his desire allows him, in an upside-down hypnosis, to embody the hypnotized patient" (273). Instead of being the cause of idealization and fascination, the analyst has to accept being subjected to the primary processes of the patient.[103]In fact, for Lacan, the key to psychoanalytic technique is for the analyst to let his or her desire remain unexpressed and unknowable: "It is in as much as the analyst's desire, which remains an x, tends in a direction that is the exact opposite of identification, that the crossing of the plane of identification is possible … " (274). This call to keep the analyst's desire unknown contrasts with the current model of the analyst or therapist revealing their own thoughts and feelings.[104]

In Lacan's return to Freud's fundamental concepts, we have seen the close relation between theory and practice, and while some critics think Lacan is an intellectual whose obscure theories are divorced from clinical realities, his work can help us to understand the reasons and potential pitfalls of analytic technique. However, I have also revealed the problematic way that Lacan confuses the unconscious and the primary processes and replaces the reality principle with the concept of repetition in relation to the unsymbolized real. In the next chapter, I further clarify why it is vital to understand these fundamental concepts of psychoanalysis in order to understand how to practice as an analyst.

Notes

1. Lacan, Jacques, Jacques-Alain Miller, and Alan Sheridan. *The four fundamental concepts of psycho-analysis*. Routledge, 2018.
2. Julien, Philippe. *Jacques Lacan's Return to Freud: The real, the symbolic, and the imaginary*. Vol. 2. NYU press, 1995.
3. Fink, Bruce. *The Lacanian subject: Between language and jouissance*. Princeton University Press, 1997.
4. Leader, Darian. "Lacan's myths." *The Cambridge Companion to Lacan* (2003): 35–49.
5. Thom, Martin. "The unconscious structured as a language." *The talking cure*. Palgrave Macmillan, London, 1981. 1–44.
6. Verhaeghe, Paul. "Causation and destitution of a pre-ontological non-entity: On the Lacanian subject." *Key concepts of Lacanian psychoanalysis*. Routledge, 2018. 164–189.
7. Lvi-Strauss, Claude. *The savage mind*. University of Chicago Press, 1966.
8. DiCenso, James J. "Totem and Taboo and the constitutive function of symbolic forms." *Journal of the American Academy of Religion* 64.3 (1996): 557–574.
9. Papapetros, Spyros. "Movements of the soul: traversing animism, fetishism, and the uncanny." *Discourse* 34.2–3 (2012): 185–208.
10. Lacan, Jacques, Alan Sheridan, and Malcolm Bowie. "On a question preliminary to any possible treatment of psychosis." *Ecrits*. Routledge, 2020. 198–249.
11. Grigg, Russell. "From the mechanism of psychosis to the universal condition of the symptom: on foreclosure." *Key concepts of Lacanian psychoanalysis*. Routledge, 2018. 48–74.
12. Freud, Sigmund. *Psycho-analytic notes on an autobiographical account of a case of paranoia (dementia paranoides)*. Read Books Ltd, 2014.
13. Lacan, Jacques, Jacques-Alain Ed Miller, and Russell Trans Grigg. "The seminar of Jacques Lacan, Book 3: The psychoses 1955–1956." *Translation of the seminar that Lacan delivered to the Société Française de Psychoanalyse over the course of the academic year 1955–1956*. WW Norton & Company, 1993.
14. Freud, Sigmund. *Totem And Taboo: Some Points of Agreement between the Mental Lives of Savages and*. Routledge, 2013.

15. Freud, Sigmund. "A metapsychological supplement to the theory of dreams." *The Standard Edition of the Complete Psychological Works of Sigmund Freud, Volume XIV (1914-1916): On the History of the Psycho-Analytic Movement, Papers on Metapsychology and Other Works*. 1957. 217–235.
16. Freud, Sigmund. *On narcissism: an introduction*. Read Books Ltd, 2014.
17. Apollon, Willy, Danielle Bergeron, and Lucie Cantin. *After Lacan: Clinical practice and the subject of the unconscious*. SUNY Press, 2002.
18. Freud, Sigmund, and James Strachey. *The interpretation of dreams*. New York: Gramercy Books, 1996.
19. Pavon-Cuéllar, David. "The enunciating act and the problem of the real in Lacanian discourse analysis." *Lacan, discourse, event: New psychoanalytic approaches to textual indeterminacy*. Routledge, 2013. 80–90.
20. Mehlman, Jeffrey. "The" floating signifier": from Lévi-Strauss to Lacan." *Yale French Studies* (1972): 10–37.
21. Lacan, Jacques, Jacques-Alain Ed Miller, and Bruce Trans Fink. *Desire and its interpretation: The seminar of Jacques Lacan, Book VI*. Polity Press, 2019.
22. Chessick, Richard D. "Sartre and Freud." *American journal of psychotherapy* 38.2 (1984): 229–238.
23. Grimsley, Ronald. "An aspect of Sartre and the unconscious." *Philosophy* 30.112 (1955): 33–44.
24. Freud, Sigmund, James Strachey, and Anna Freud. *The psychopathology of everyday life:(1901)*. Hogarth Press: Institute of Psycho-Analysis, 1978.
25. Wilden, Anthony G. "Freud, Signorelli, and Lacan: The Repression of the Signifier." *American Imago* 23.4 (1966): 332–366.
26. Preti, Antonio, et al. "Psychotic-like or unusual subjective experiences? The role of certainty in the appraisal of the subclinical psychotic phenotype." *Psychiatry research* 200.2–3 (2012): 669–673.
27. Soler, Colette, Esther Faye, and Susan Schwartz. *Lacan—The Unconscious Reinvented: The Unconscious Reinvented*. Routledge, 2018.
28. Boothby, Richard. *Death and Desire (RLE: Lacan): Psychoanalytic Theory in Lacan's Return to Freud*. Routledge, 2014.
29. Stavrakakis, Yannis. *Jacques Lacan*. No. IKEEBOOKCH-2020-408. Aristotle University of Thessaloniki, 2017.
30. Lacan, Jacques, Alan Sheridan, and Malcolm Bowie. "The Subversion of the Subject and the Dialectic of Desire in the Freudian Unconscious." *Écrits*. Routledge, 2020. 323–360.

31. Rajchman, John. *Truth and Eros: Foucault, Lacan and the question of ethics*. Routledge, 2013.
32. Samuels, Robert. "Science and the reality principle." *Freud for the twenty-first century*. Palgrave Pivot, Cham, 2019. 5–16.
33. Botting, Fred. "Relations of the Real in Lacan, Bataille and Blanchot." *SubStance* 23.1 (1994): 24–40.
34. Zupancic, Alenka. *Ethics of the real: Kant and Lacan*. Verso Trade, 2011.
35. Kran, Anne. "Comparing causality in Freudian reasoning and critical realism." *Journal of Critical Realism* 9.1 (2010): 5–32.
36. Bistoen, Gregory, Stijn Vanheule, and Stef Craps. "Nachträglichkeit: A Freudian perspective on delayed traumatic reactions." *Theory & Psychology* 24.5 (2014): 668–687.
37. Cardoso, Mauricio José d'Escragnolle, and Rosane Zétola Lustoza. "From Freudian representation to Lacanian signifying: the pertinence of structural interpretation of the unconscious." *Psicologia: Teoria e Pesquisa* 28.2 (2012): 219–226.
38. Plotnitsky, Arkady. "On Lacan and mathematics." *Œuvres & Critiques* 34.2 (2009): 143–162.
39. Freud, Sigmund. "Repression." *The Standard Edition of the Complete Psychological Works of Sigmund Freud, Volume XIV (1914-1916): On the History of the Psycho-Analytic Movement, Papers on Metapsychology and Other Works*. 1957. 141–158.
40. Shepherdson, Charles. *Lacan and the Limits of Language*. Fordham University Press, 2009.
41. Freud, Sigmund. *Totem And Taboo: Some Points of Agreement between the Mental Lives of Savages and*. Routledge, 2013.
42. Stavrakakis, Yannis. *Jacques Lacan*. No. IKEEBOOKCH-2020-408. Aristotle University of Thessaloniki, 2017.
43. Gutiérrez-Peláez, Miguel. "Ferenczi's anticipation of the traumatic dimension of language: A meeting with Lacan." *Contemporary Psychoanalysis* 51.1 (2015): 137–154.
44. Gutiérrez-Peláez, Miguel. "Ferenczi's anticipation of the traumatic dimension of language: A meeting with Lacan." *Contemporary Psychoanalysis* 51.1 (2015): 137–154.
45. Kesner, Ladislav. "Wandering or unhappy mind?." *American Journal of Psychiatry* 171.9 (2014): 929–930.
46. Bowie, Malcolm. *Lacan*. Harvard University Press, 1993.

47. Muller, John, P. "Ego and subject in Lacan." *Psychoanalytic review* 69.2 (1982): 234–240.
48. McIntosh, Donald. "The ego and the self in the thought of Sigmund Freud." *International journal of psycho-analysis* 67 (1986): 429–448.
49. Rosa, Carmelo Licitra, et al. "From the Imaginary to Theory of the Gaze in Lacan." *Frontiers in Psychology* 12 (2021).
50. Lacan, Jacques. "The mirror stage as formative of the function of the I as revealed in psychoanalytic experience." *Écrits: a selection* (2001): 146–178.
51. Bernet, Rudolf. "The Phenomenon of the Gaze in Merleau-Ponty and Lacan." *Chiasmi International* 1 (1999): 105–118.
52. Barnes, Jenny. "Phenomenological intentionality meets an ego-less state." *Indo-Pacific Journal of Phenomenology* 3.1 (2003): 1–17.
53. Brennan, Teresa, and Martin Jay. *Vision in context: historical and contemporary perspectives on sight*. Routledge, 2013.
54. Lacan, Jacques. *The Ego in Freud's Theory and in the Technique of Psychoanalysis, 1954-1955*. Vol. 2. WW Norton & Company, 1991.
55. Samuels, Robert. "Vertigo: Sexual disorientation and the engendering of the real." *Gender and Psychoanalysis* 5.1 (2000): 81–97.
56. Krips, Henry. "The politics of the gaze: Foucault, Lacan and Žižek." *Culture Unbound* 2.1 (2010): 91–102.
57. Malin, Barnet D. "Kohut and Lacan: mirror opposites." *Psychoanalytic Inquiry* 31.1 (2011): 58–74.
58. Smith, Joseph H. *Arguing with Lacan: Ego psychology and language*. Yale University Press, 1991.
59. McGowan, Todd. "Looking for the gaze: Lacanian film theory and its vicissitudes." *Cinema Journal* (2003): 27–47.
60. Samuels, Robert. *Between philosophy and psychoanalysis: Lacan's reconstruction of Freud*. Routledge, 2014.
61. Bonomi, Carlo. "Narcissism as mastered visibility: The evil eye and the attack of the disembodied gaze." *International Forum of Psychoanalysis*. Vol. 19. No. 2. Taylor & Francis Group, 2010.
62. McGowan, Todd. *The real gaze: Film theory after Lacan*. SUNY Press, 2012.
63. Purser, Ronald E. "A Buddhist–Lacanian perspective on lack." *The Humanistic Psychologist* 39.4 (2011): 289.
64. Feldstein, Richard, Bruce Fink, and Maire Jaanus, eds. *Reading Seminar XI: Lacan's Four Fundamental Concepts of Psychoanalysis: The Paris Seminars in English*. SUNY Press, 1995.

65. Freud, Sigmund. "Remembering, repeating and working-through (Further recommendations on the technique of psycho-analysis II)." *The Standard Edition of the Complete Psychological Works of Sigmund Freud, Volume XII (1911-1913): The Case of Schreber, Papers on Technique and Other Works*. 1958. 145–156.
66. Cottet, Serge. "Should we analyse the transference." *Journal of the Centre for Freudian Analysis and Research* 2 (1993): 3–10.
67. Nobus, Dany. *Jacques Lacan and the Freudian practice of psychoanalysis*. Routledge, 2013.
68. Fink, Bruce. *Fundamentals of psychoanalytic technique: A Lacanian approach for practitioners*. WW Norton & Company, 2007.
69. Fink, Bruce. *Lacan on Love: An Exploration of Lacan's Seminar VIII, Transference*. John Wiley & Sons, 2015.
70. Freud, Sigmund. "Group psychology and the analysis of the ego." *The Standard Edition of the Complete Psychological Works of Sigmund Freud, Volume XVIII (1920-1922): Beyond the Pleasure Principle, Group Psychology and Other Works*. 1955. 65–144.
71. Ruti, Mari. "The fall of fantasies: A Lacanian reading of lack." *Journal of the American Psychoanalytic Association* 56.2 (2008): 483–508.
72. Etchegoyen, R. Horacio. "The dialectics of the transference according to Lacan." *The Fundamentals of Psychoanalytic Technique*. Routledge, 2018. 114–126.
73. Lacan, Jacques. "Remarque sur le rapport de Daniel Lagache: Psychanalyse et structure de la personnalité." *Écrits* (1966): 647–684.
74. Hanly, Charles. "Ego ideal and ideal ego." *International journal of psycho-analysis* 65 (1984): 253–261.
75. Shepherdson, Charles. *Vital signs: Nature, culture, psychoanalysis*. Routledge, 2002.
76. Luepnitz, Deborah. "Beyond the phallus: Lacan and feminism." *The Cambridge Companion to Lacan* (2003): 221–237.
77. Zupancic, Alenka. *What is sex?*. MIT Press, 2017.
78. Sauvagnat, François. "Notes on the Evolution of the Relationship between Guilt and Shame in Psychoanalysis and Anthropology." *Revista Latinoamericana de Psicopatologia Fundamental* 21 (2018): 779–797.
79. Hook, Derek. "Tracking the Lacanian unconscious in language." *Psychodynamic Practice* 19.1 (2013): 38–54.
80. MacIntyre, Alasdair Chalmers. *The unconscious: a conceptual analysis*. Routledge, 2004.

81. Braunstein, Néstor. "Desire and Jouissance in the Teachings of Lacan." *The Cambridge Companion to Lacan* (2003): 102–115.
82. Kim, Jin Sook. "Symbolic death of the subject in the structure of Jacques Lacan." *Death, Dying, and Mysticism*. Palgrave Macmillan, New York, 2015. 103–115.
83. Swales, Stephanie S. *Perversion: A Lacanian psychoanalytic approach to the subject*. Routledge, 2012.
84. Baldwin, Yael Goldman. *Lacan and addiction: An anthology*. Routledge, 2018.
85. Braunstein, Néstor. "Desire and Jouissance in the Teachings of Lacan." *The Cambridge Companion to Lacan* (2003): 102–115.
86. Compton, Allan. "On the Psychoanalytic Theory of Instinctual Drives: I: The Beginnings of Freud's Drive Theory." *The Psychoanalytic Quarterly* 50.2 (1981): 190–218.
87. Freud, Sigmund. "Fetishism." *The Standard Edition of the Complete Psychological Works of Sigmund Freud, Volume XXI (1927-1931): The Future of an Illusion, Civilization and its Discontents, and Other Works*. 1961. 147–158.
88. Freud, Sigmund. "Fetishism." *The Standard Edition of the Complete Psychological Works of Sigmund Freud, Volume XXI (1927-1931): The Future of an Illusion, Civilization and its Discontents, and Other Works*. 1961. 147–158.
89. Verbeke, Evi. "The Self-Destructive Body through the Lens of Foucault and Lacan." *The Body in Theory: Essays After Lacan and Foucault* (2021): 56.
90. New, ANTONIA S., and Joseph Triebwasser. "A history of borderline personality disorder." *Borderline Personality Disorder* (2017): 1.
91. Nurnberg, H. George, et al. "Evaluation of diagnostic criteria for borderline personality disorder." *American Journal of Psychiatry* 145.10 (1988): 1280–1284.
92. Keiser, Sylvan. "Body ego during orgasm." *The Psychoanalytic Quarterly* 21.2 (1952): 153–166.
93. Samuels, Robert. "Transference and Narcissism." *Freud for the Twenty-First Century*. Palgrave Pivot, Cham, 2019. 43–51.
94. Moncayo, Raul. *Evolving Lacanian perspectives for clinical psychoanalysis: On narcissism, sexuation, and the phases of analysis in contemporary culture*. Routledge, 2018.

95. Fink, Bruce. "Freud and Lacan on love: A preliminary exploration." *Filozofski vestnik* 25.2 (2004).
96. Samuels, Robert. "Beyond Hillary Clinton: Obsessional Narcissism and the Failure of the Liberal Class." *Psychoanalyzing the Left and Right after Donald Trump*. Palgrave Macmillan, Cham, 2016. 31–59.
97. Samuels, Robert. "(Liberal) Narcissism." *Routledge Handbook of Psychoanalytic Political Theory*. Routledge, 2019. 151–161.
98. Schwartz, Susan. "The golem of narcissism." *Analysis* 22 (2019): 145–150.
99. Schleifer, Ronald. "Lacan's enunciation and the cure of mortality: Teaching, transference, and desire." *College English*49.7 (1987): 801–815.
100. Adorno, Theodor W. "Freudian theory and the pattern of fascist propaganda." *The essential Frankfurt school reader*(1982): 118–137.
101. Macalpine, Ida. "The development of the transference." *The Psychoanalytic Quarterly* 19.4 (1950): 501–539.
102. Chertok, Léon, and Isabelle Stengers. *A critique of psychoanalytic reason: Hypnosis as a scientific problem from Lavoisier to Lacan*. Stanford University Press, 1992.
103. Bracher, Mark. "How analysis cures according to Lacan." *The subject of Lacan: A Lacanian reader for psychologists* (2000): 189–208.
104. Fink, Bruce. *A clinical introduction to Lacanian psychoanalysis: Theory and technique*. Harvard University Press, 1999.

5

The Desire of the Analyst and the American Repression of Psychoanalysis

In looking at two post-Freudian thinkers, I have examined how psychoanalysis is being (mis)understood within analysis itself. To further clarify what shapes these misunderstandings and what is at stake in this repression of Freud's fundamental concepts, I will interpret Mitchell Wilson's *The Analyst Desire*.[1] I am choosing this book because Wilson is a mainstream American analyst who also has a deep interest in Lacan. However, my main focus will be on how an incorrect understanding of Freud's theory results in a questionable analytic technique.

The Ethics of Care

One of the framing metaphors that Wilson uses throughout his book is the idea that the analyst acts as a host or inn keeper for the patient: "While the analyst is a gracious host—and part of that grace is knowing that she will inevitably reveal some of her own concerns and desires to her charge—her attention and concern are directed to the patient for his benefit. The vector of ethical responsibility goes in one direction" (16). By arguing that the ethical responsibility in analysis belongs solely to the

R. Samuels, *(Mis)Understanding Freud with Lacan, Zizek, and Neuroscience*, The Palgrave Lacan Series, https://doi.org/10.1007/978-3-031-13327-5_5

analyst, Wilson presents a non-psychoanalytic notion of ethics because he fails to see how the central responsibility of the patient is to speak without censoring in order to discover the truth of their inner and outer reality.[2] Likewise, the analyst's main desire is for the patient to free associate, and this is accomplished by the analyst remaining neutral.[3] The ethical responsibility of the analyst and the patient therefore rely on a certain faith in the analytic process.

In order to remain neutral, it is essential for the analyst to take on a position of self-effacement, which may appear to be cold and impersonal, but it is necessary for the working through of the transference.[4] Since the patient comes to analysis with a fundamental demand for love, recognition, and understanding, the non-response of the analyst allows for these unconscious desires to emerge. However, as Lacan warns, if the analyst takes on the position of the one who knows or cares, then the patient will be unable to recognize and then overcome these underlying unconscious forces.[5] Yet, it appears that like so many other analysts and therapists, Wilson does not accept the position of the analyst as he posits the need to be kind, comforting, and understanding: "Anything might be said. Dialogue is implicit, even if the analyst is silent in her response. There is the direct discourse of positive content: 'This happened, and that happened. I feel this way and that way'—the normal currency of conversational relating between parties. There develops 'the bond of safe company,' the comfort born of the analyst's reliable kindness, willingness to speak truthfully, and to meet consistently" (16–17). What Wilson appears to miss here is that psychoanalysis is an artificial relationship unlike any other mode of communication.[6] In fact, one of the major reasons why someone goes to a psychoanalyst is because friends and family have not been able to help with the patient's symptoms; in order to make a change, a very different type of relationship has to be established, and yet many analysts resist this difference.

Wilson's resistance to analysis itself can be seen in his description of the basic responsibilities of the patient and the analyst: "while the patient has two clear commitments—to come to the agreed-upon sessions and to pay the analyst for them—as I said earlier, the vector of care and responsibility goes in one direction, from analyst to patient" (18). What Wilson leaves out from this description is the responsibility of the patient to follow the fundamental rule, which is free association. Moreover, the analyst is responsible for suspending judgment so that the patient can also do the same.[7] This is clearly not an everyday relationship, and that is why it is so important to understand the theory supporting the practice of psychoanalysis.

Although it is sometimes necessary to deviate from strict analytic neutrality, it is vital to realize how the analytic process can be easily subverted when the analyst refuses to play the required role.[8] In fact, Wilson appears to disregard these foundations of analytic practice in the following passage: "Over the years I have had occasion to drive patients from my office to doctors' offices and emergency rooms. I have made phone calls on their behalf that they could not. I have had them bring their computers to the office to do work that had otherwise been languishing for months or longer. And I have been known to prepare a cup of tea or two" (18). Instead of performing the optimal frustration of the patient's drives, Wilson wants to be experienced as a caring host and helper.[9] The major problem with this approach is that not only does one feed the demands of the patient, but once one steps away from the position of being an empty mirror, it is difficult to return to being a blank screen. Since the analyst wants the content of the transference to come from the patient's imagination, any disclosures by the analyst taints the process.[10]

To be clear, as we shall see, the analyst cannot remain completely silent or passive, but the interventions have to be directed towards the goal of free association and the neutralizing of the artificial transference relationship. The trick is how to interpret without being the subject who is supposed to know or the moral authority.[11] Unfortunately, the difficulty of maintaining this analytic position has been increased because theorists like Wilson want to base their practice of therapy on the model of being a good mother: "All of these aspects of practice fall under the umbrella of the matricial. Matricial space is the phrase that to me best captures the background conditions that facilitate—that hold, flexibly, steadily—the ongoing conversational engagement that is psychoanalysis" (18). In this focus on the analyst taking on the attributes of a good mother, Wilson and others seek to envision analytic treatment as a form of reparative parenting.[12] As Lacan insists, one of the problems with this model is that it only serves to feed the narcissistic demand for love, understanding, and recognition.[13] Since the ideal ego wants to be recognized by the ego ideal while repressing the super-ego, the re-enactment of the good mother relationship functions to strengthen the ego's defenses.[14] In Oedipal terms, this form of therapy seeks to symbolically kill off the father in order to maintain the love of the mother. However, what Wilson and others do not realize is that in order for analysis to progress, the narcissistic transference has to be revealed and called into question.[15]

In a very telling passage, Wilson traces his analytic position to a theory of maternal care that appears to function to extend the Oedipus complex:

> The phrase matricial space, and the theorization of it, comes from Viviane Chetrit-Vatine. Her book, *The Ethical Seduction of the Analytic Situation* (2014), is an extended investigation into the strangeness and risk that inhere in any meaningful encounter with the other. The foundational encounter with the other is the mother/caretaker in relation to her/his/their child; the psychoanalytic encounter evokes and re-figures this original relational moment. (33–34)

While Freud stressed the conflicted nature of human relationships, Wilson turns to the figure of the all-loving mother in order to argue that the analyst should desire to be this idealized care-giver.[16] One possible reason for this misunderstanding of psychoanalytic theory and practice is the growing dominance of certain feminist perspectives within the general culture and analysis itself.[17] In response to the perception that Freud saw the identification with the father as the solution to all social and personal problems, many analysts and therapists have sought to emphasize the role played by the mother; however, what should be clear from Freud's work is that the analyst has to resist playing any role, especially a parental one.[18]

Wilson believes that the analyst should embody a caring mother because unlike other animals, humans are highly dependent on caregivers for an extended period of time: "These conditions are all the more acutely present within the context of what Jean Laplanche (1999) calls the primary anthropological situation of infancy, that radically dependent relation between the infans, the helpless infant, and the adult caretaker. The psychoanalytic situation recapitulates the primary one, and so, like the primary caregivers of a small child, the analyst is in a position of ethical responsibility for the other, her patient" (19). As I have pointed out in previous chapters, this fundamental relationship of dependency is at the center of Freud's theory of transference, but the goal of analysis is to work through this relationship and not reinforce it. In short, the ethics of psychoanalysis is directed towards the discovery of the truth of reality and not the recreation of an idealized relationship of dependency where the responsibility for meeting unmet needs is transferred from the subject to the Other.[19]

It is important to point out that many feminist psychoanalysts have critiqued Freud's focus on separation and independence because they see it as a masculine, anti-social desire predicated on promoting the competitive masculine individualist of modern capitalism.[20] What these critiques often fail to understand is that the neutrality of the analyst and the free association of the analysand are founded on suspending judgment and allowing for the subject to explore the effects of all ideologies and identities.[21] The analyst simply does not take sides or try to take on the role of being a mother or father; instead, a space is cleared for the patient to explore how these social and political norms and values have shaped their existence.[22] Unfortunately, Wilson cannot accept the neutrality of the analyst, and so he continues to equate this position with a series of social role models:

> For the patient, the physicianly analyst is a powerful activator of the transference neurosis and the working alliance. The patient's image of the doctor stirs up memories, fantasies, and feelings from childhood of an authoritative, arbitrary, incomprehensible, and magical figure who possessed the power of the omnipotent, omniscient parents. It is the doctor who takes over when the parents are sick and afraid. It is the doctor who has the right to explore the naked body, and who has no fear or disgust of blood, mucus, vomit, urine, or feces. He is the rescuer from pain and panic, the establisher of order from chaos, provider of emergency functions performed by the mother in the first years of life. In addition, the physician inflicts pain, pierces the flesh, and intrudes into every opening in the body. He is reminiscent of the mother of bodily intimacy as well as the representative of the sadomasochistic fantasies involving both parents. (19–20)

This equation of the analyst with the caring doctor goes against Freud's idea that medicine wants nothing to do with the unconscious, hysterical symptoms, or the unconscious.[23] In fact, when the patient places the analyst in the position of the caring physician, the idealizing transference is not only activated but it becomes reinforced as one chooses the cure of love over the cure of analysis.[24] Wilson simply resists seeing how his theory and practice end up feeding the transference instead of clearing a space to work through it.

Although it is very tempting and gratifying for the analyst to feel idealized by the patient, this type of relationship serves to re-enforce the transference in an imaginary manner.[25] As Lacan has pointed out, when the patient idealizes the analyst, the patient places the Other in the position of the ego ideal, which then is manipulated to recognize and verify the patient's self-idealization.[26] Like someone who is addicted to placing pictures of themselves on the Web so others can "like" their image, the desire to be recognized by an idealized spectator feeds the unconscious demand for control and satisfaction.[27] Instead of recognizing the pathological nature of idealization in analysis, Wilson expresses how good it feels to be admired by his patient: "Relationally, Paul feels relieved that I showed I had survived his attacks, and did it in a way that reached him, and also in a way that he could admire" (24). In this representation of the dual relation between the analyst and the patient, the patient admires the analyst who is able to tolerate aggression; however, we have to ask if this conception of analysis enables free association and the discovery of unconscious content.[28] From Lacan's perspective, it is a mistake to see the analytic relation in a dualistic manner because this type of structure locks both subjects into an imaginary world of envy, rivalry, identification, and idealization.[29]

To break out from this imaginary dualism, the analyst has to refrain from feeding the transference by remaining neutral and impersonal. Clearly, this type of position goes against our natural tendency to care for the other and make immediate problems go away, and yet, the only way for someone to discover something new is if they stop acting in a natural or intuitive manner. The power of psychoanalysis, then, is that is offers a new type of relationship that is radically different from other forms of social interaction, and this means that the patient should always experience an analytic session as something strange and different.[30]

Comforting the Patient

However, the strangeness of the unconscious and the analytic relationship is often repressed in many forms of therapy because the therapists seek to bring immediate comfort to their patients. Wilson describes this therapeutic impulse in the following manner: "Through this repurposing of speech the strange is then made more familiar" (27). Rather than seeing analysis as the discovery of something new and different, Wilson stresses the way language can be used to make the strange appear familiar. In other words, analysis becomes a method for repression as unconscious material is translated into the discourse of normal communication.[31]

As an effort to be a good host and a loving mother for his patients, Wilson reverses Lacan's insistence that the analyst take on the position of impersonality: "Lacan was right to lay claim to the speech relation and its structuring effects as the central organizing endeavor of psychoanalysis. He was simply wrong, to be blunt about it, in so vigorously cautioning the analyst to refuse the personal engagement, and to view with great skepticism any attention paid to the qualities of the therapeutic relationship, reducing—in his terms—the subject to an ego" (30). In arguing against the neutrality of the analyst, Wilson reveals how he borrows psychoanalytic terms from Lacan and Freud, but he removes their original intent so that they now have an opposing meaning. In fact, the title of his book is derived from Lacan's theory of the desire of the analyst, which is very telling because Wilson presents a radical misunderstanding of what Lacan meant by this term.[32]

What Wilson and others fail to accept is the idea that desire is always for something one does not have, and so when Lacan refers to the desire of the analyst, he is not referring to something that the analyst knows or possess.[33] Instead, the analyst's desire remains an unknown variable for the patient, which then becomes a source for fantasy, transference, and projection. Lacan may say that the desire of the analyst is for absolute difference, but this definition only reiterates the presence of an absence.[34]

As the unknowable object causing the patient to desire, the analyst is a cause and not a goal or value.[35] Moreover, by resisting identification and idealization, the analyst clears a space for the patient's free discovery of unconscious material. In fact, Wilson does at times recognize this need for the analyst to break out of a narcissistic relation with the self and the other: "Any position the analyst maintains, especially one based on psychoanalytic theory that one avers to the true—really believes in, and really thinks is right in the veridical sense of the word—can fall prey to excessive narcissistic investment, and serve the purposes of shoring up the analyst's wavering ego. The analyst's desire is always a position contrary to her narcissism in whatever form that investment takes" (33). If in narcissism, the subject wants the idealized self-image to be verified and recognized by an idealized Other or cultural ideal, then it is vital for the analyst to suspend this imaginary mode of relating.[36]

Writing about Analysis

Just as Freud realized that the recounting of a dream is always being revised through the secondary processes, Wilson affirms that when an analyst is discussing a case, the narrative places the analyst in the position of the hero: "The writer-analyst is not only representing her work in the vignette (i.e., what "really happened"), she is also a character in the story that she is telling. By depicting the analyst as both a clever sleuth and a determined healer, the reader is invited to admire (and identify with) the analyst qua analyst, while perhaps not appreciating that the machinery of rhetorical persuasion is being used to effect this admiration and identification" (44). Wilson highlights here one reason why it is so hard to write about analysis: the narrative structure of presenting a case tends to rewrite history by placing the analyst in the position of the ego ideal in a transference relationship with the reader.[37] In this structure, complexity, ambiguity, ambivalence, and ignorance are repressed so that the narrator can be seen as the hero of the story.

Since the narcissistic ego wants to be seen as the one who knows, psychoanalysis itself has to be distorted and repressed in the recounting of cases:

> It is common for all analysts, at various points in a psychoanalytic treatment, to see ourselves in precisely these ways: in the face of obstacles both obscure and obvious, the analyst is a determined and at times clever healer who pieces together new ways of understanding and explaining the patient's symptoms and predicaments. This picture is not only promoted by our clinical literature, it is an alluring one for the clinical psychoanalyst, who, as I have described in this chapter, is in no way exempt from the vagaries and wavering of the ego and its narcissistic struggles. (44)

One reason for this analytic struggle is that analysts refuse to accept taking on a position of neutrality, and so they fall into the "normal" way of relating, knowing, and communicating. As Wilson points out, it is hard for someone to give up the admiration for being the clever one who can figure out what others have failed to understand. Furthermore, Wilson is correct in positing that the narrative form itself pushes analysts to distort the experience of psychoanalysis: "First, to the extent that the analyst identifies herself with the hero/detective image she will tend to invest, and perhaps overly commit to, the explanatory narrative that is being constructed in the analysis. The second reason has to do with the nature of narrative itself: narrative explanations tend to create their own demands for coherence as they get built" (44–45). As a discourse of discovery, psychoanalysis does not lend itself to narrative closure or self-satisfied understanding. For instance, if the patient is able to speak without censoring or self-reflection, then the produced discourse will often be fragmented, incoherent, and de-idealized.[38]

Wilson himself does recognize that our desire for understanding and narrative order can serve to undermine the very discourse the analyst is trying to represent:

> If we are too interested in "connecting the dots," then moments of newness, surprise, oddity, confusion, contradiction, and repetition tend to get ignored or devalued. In fact, the psychoanalyst ought to be biased toward narrative's disruption, against which something new and different can be appreciated. While we all do this story-building to some extent, it is hazardous to make it the central focus of the analysis. (46)

There is then a radical disconnect between the discourse of free association and the narrative retelling of an analytic case, and this distinction leads to the misunderstanding of psychoanalysis.[39] In fact, one reason why one needs to go through analysis to be an analyst is that the only way one can really learn about psychoanalysis is through experience.

The difficulty in teaching psychoanalysis as a traditional academic discipline is related to this need for analytic experience and the working through of the transference. Unlike other instructional relationships, the analyst has to refrain from being the one who knows, and this refusal of identification is hard to maintain. As Freud discovered early on, if you simply interpret a patient's symptoms or resistances, these issues will continue to return: what is necessary is for the patient to make the discovery on their own concerning the causes of their problems. The analyst still needs to intervene to keep the process going, but these interventions should not feed the idea that the analyst has all of the answers. Moreover, Freud was dedicated to seeing free association as a path towards individual autonomy, and so he stopped trying to tell his patients what to think and say.[40]

From Hypnosis to Neutrality

The development of Freud's technique can be traced from his early use of hypnosis to his later employment of free association.[41] By moving from a position of being the master who tells the patient what to think to the position of neutrality, Freud discovered what enables the patient the ability to speak without judgment. As we shall see, Wilson both accepts and rejects this emphasis on the analyst being neutral and suspending all judgment and knowledge: "The patient doesn't know that he doesn't want to know the difficult thing, the unwanted desire, the hateful or shameful feeling, especially in the presence of the analyst. This twofold 'not wanting to know' analysts called resistance. The analyst's job, in this view, is to 'analyze the patient's resistances,' so that they become more familiar to the person who deploys them" (50). The problem with analyzing the resistances is that the analyst falls back into the position of being the master who knows and judges. While it appears to be much easier and direct to tell patients about their defenses, this type of intervention only serves to heighten the transference and strengthen the resistances of the ego.[42]

A frustrating aspect of Wilson's book is that at times he does seem to understand the need for analytic neutrality, but at other times, he argues against it. For example, in the following passage, we see how the desire of the analyst can result in establishing a dual relationship of opposition between the patient's ego and the analyst's ego: "Here is Friedman again, in another part of his discussion, more forceful and direct: 'There's a demand for work here ... a bending of purpose, a conflict of wills, a verdict of satisfactoriness. The analyst is not just a facilitator; he is a taskmaster and judge' (1993, 13). Yes, a demand, a conflict, a verdict. That captures things better. Resistance has no meaning unless there is a force pushing against it" (52–53). In seeing the analyst as a judge and taskmaster, the neutrality of the position is eliminated as one takes on the role of super-ego or ego-ideal.[43] This type of analytic relationship can only function to increase the resistances of the ego and reinforce the transference, and so it is necessary to couple analytic training with a theory devised to protect against faulty analytic interventions.

Theory and Practice

In other words, we need to teach psychoanalysis and write and speak about it in order to clearly define the role of the analyst.[44] Although psychoanalytic theory also has important things to say about human psychology and culture, the training of analysts requires a clear understanding of transference, repression, the pleasure principle, the primary processes, and the reality principle. On the most basic level, analysts have to understand how transference enables the repression of the primary processes in order to satisfy the pleasure principle, and the only way to attain the reality principle is through the neutrality of the analyst causing the free association of the patient. In fact, this concept of neutrality represents the heart of modern science and democratic law because we want our scientists to look at evidence without prejudice just as we want our judges to judge without bias.[45] Neutrality is then a key invention of the modern

Enlightenment, and as a necessary but impossible ideal, it is never fully attained, and yet we desire to fulfil this ideal to the best of our ability.[46]

In the movement from the pleasure principle to the reality principle, it is essential to suspend judgment and eliminate all prejudices and biases; however, as we have seen in Wilson's discourse, this practice of neutrality is very hard to maintain. One reason for this difficulty is the way our egos seek to maintain a positive self-image by idealizing the knowledge of the self and the other:[47]

> resistances have to do with the stickiness of bias, a self-protective effort to maintain one's position, one's self-esteem, one's identity in the face of uncertainly or threat. Kohut (1971) deserves full credit for putting narcissism on the psychoanalytic map as a central aspect of normative psychosocial development, rather than a pathological manifestation of that development gone awry. Lacan, however different he is from Kohut in other respects, also theorized a normal narcissism through his concept of the mirror stage and the structuring of the ego by way of a series of identifications. (53)

In linking bias to the resistances of the narcissistic ego, Wilson reveals the limits of his own discourse. As much as he would like to maintain the position of analytic neutrality, he cannot help interpreting his patents' resistances and substantiating the desire of the analyst.

The Known Desire of the Analyst

While Lacan insists that the analyst's desire must remain an unknown variable and cause, Wilson, like so many other analysts and therapists, wants to define this desire through theory and personality: "Regarding the analyst's desire, it can be seen or glimpsed within the various actions that desire motivates, including why each of us chooses to be an analyst (see Chap. 1), our theoretical persuasions, and the kinds of experiences we want to have with our patients for our own particular reasons" (57). This notion that the analyst shapes the analytic relation based on theoretical persuasion and particular reasons goes against the need for the analyst to suspend judgment and eliminate all bias. Instead of seeing the practice of psychoanalysis as shaped by different competing theories, I have stressed the need to return to Freud's fundamental concepts as a way of protecting against misunderstanding the role of the analyst.

Of course, in the age of postmodern relativism, it may appear absurd to insist that there is a single way to understand Freud and psychoanalysis; however, it is vital to insist on the validity of his initial insights in relation to the development of his technique.[48] In fact, I have been arguing that five key concepts structure the field itself, and any misunderstanding of these notions results in deviations in the practice of analysis. Yet, many therapists and analysts will resist this argument because they simply do not understand these foundational principles and the process of analysis itself. It is also difficult to critique the analyst as the one who knows and then present a theory and practice with a strict set of definitions. Just as the Enlightenment seeks to promote a bias against bias, the privileging of neutrality is itself a value that has to be defended through the use of non-neutral concepts.[49]

Returning to Wilson's discussion of the analyst, we see how psychoanalytic theory and practice has been shaped by a continuous resistance to analytic neutrality:

> Once upon a time, many analysts—whether ego psychological or Kleinian—claimed that the analyst's wishes for certain experiences represent unresolved neurotic conflict. In this picture, the well-analyzed analyst was "neutral" and her work was burdened, at most, by a few well-understood "blind spots." This state of affairs is an obvious impossibility, because the analyst's wishing is inevitable, her pushing and prodding—however tactful, however gentle—ubiquitous, and her exercising of judgment on the proceedings a central part of her ethical position. The picture of the "well-analyzed" analyst is, then, itself wishful, and points to a fantasy of wholeness, integration, and plentitude, and, at the same time an elision of our basic lacking and desiring state. To believe one is "well-analyzed" is to live in one version of a narcissistic enclosure, precisely what Laplanche warned us about. (57–58)

As Wilson indicates, one of the reasons why analysts have to undergo their own analysis is that they need to learn how to overcome their biases when they work with patients. However, Wilson dismisses this goal of neutrality as a narcissistic fantasy as he returns to the misguided notion that the analyst cannot stop judging and wanting specific things in relation to patients.[50] Here, we see how psychoanalysis becomes repressed within analysis itself as key concepts are misunderstood and then discarded.

On the one hand, Wilson does follow Lacan in affirming that desire is always based on loss and lack, but on the other hand, he keeps positing that specific desires shape the actions of the analyst.[51] It is simply too tempting to fall into non-psychoanalytic understandings of desire, knowledge, and communication, and so the practice of analysis is itself avoided. This misunderstanding of psychoanalysis is evident in Wilson's view of reason and rationality: "Psychoanalysts have struggled with the proposition—though I believe we might as well call it a fact of human being—that our cherished "rationality" is shot through with self-interest. Aristotle argued that what makes human beings human is their capacity for rational activity, the putting to use of practical reason in the undertaking of various goal-directed actions" (58). Wilson connects reason and rationality to self-interest, but Freud's theory of the reality principle and Descartes' conception of modern science rely on the possibility of suspending self-interest in the quest to separate the real from the fictional.[52] For Freud, one of the central tasks of the reality principle is to counter the tendency of human thought to confuse internalized memories with perceptions of the external world.[53] As a way of breaking free from the pleasure principle and the primary processes, one has to give up on the omnipotence of thought through the process of reality testing. In other words, Freud takes the ideal of reason derived from Enlightenment philosophy and science and applies it to everyday experience.[54] Through free association, one learns to approach the reality of one's own mind without bias or self-interest.

As Wilson points out, the ego psychologists did attempt to emphasize the reality principle, but they failed to separate this form of reason from the rationalizations and secondary revisions of the defensive ego:

> American ego psychologists (Hartmann, for one) tended to highlight the ego's rational capacities, and they insisted on a distinction between the ego and the self. Hartmann (1950) writes: "It therefore will be clarifying if we define narcissism as the libidinal cathexis not of the ego but of the self" (85). Why would Hartmann want to make this separation? Because in doing so the ego is more or less cleansed of narcissistic needs and the influences of the drives (sex and aggression). With the advent of the structural model, the theoretical status of the ego changed: it was now conceptualized as a set of functions that gained an autonomy from the internal, thereby allowing it, so the Hartmannian story went, to adapt healthily to the world relatively unburdened by internal exigencies and pressures. (58)

Lacan critiques this development of ego psychology in psychoanalysis because he believes that the separation of the ego from narcissism makes no sense since the ego is developed and sustained through narcissism.[55] Lacan also critiques the way that many ego psychologists saw the end of analysis as centered on the patient identifying with the reality testing of the analyst.[56] Lacan argues that this identification is a form of alienation and a prolongation of the transference; however, I would argue that the ego psychologists were onto something when they sought to place the responsibility for reality testing in an internal agency outside of narcissism.

If psychoanalysis requires coming to terms with the inner truth of one's fantasies, unconscious thoughts, and primary processes, then it is necessary to posit a source for internal reality testing. However, with the turn against neutrality inside and outside of psychoanalysis, the possibility for an unbiased approach to the real is eliminated. Wilson, himself, repeats this problem by arguing against the ideal of a non-biased, objective perspective: "In other words, there is an inherently self-validating aspect to thinking and perceiving … Opatow's work gives us yet another angle on the ego functions of rationality and judgment: there is no such thing as 'neutral' thinking" (59). By rejecting the necessary but impossible ideal of neutral thinking, Wilson gives up on the possibility of the reality principle and the ability to see psychoanalysis as a science. Although it is important to focus on how the ego seeks self-validation in its perceptions and thoughts, it is also vital to affirm that the neutrality of the analyst and the free association of the patient open up the space for a move beyond pure self-interest.

It is also essential to point out that for Freud, thought structured by the primary processes is often delusional because it is not tied to reality and cannot be controlled by the ego.[57] Psychoanalysis, then, has to provide a critique of pure thought as it calls for the separation of representations from reality, yet Wilson claims that thinking is by definition narcissistic and self-serving: "Thinking is suffused with a distinctly narcissistic, self-aggrandizing desire. I hope it is clear by this point that I do not mean to imply something pathological in using the term 'narcissistic.' Thinking is a self-preservative function, and in that very important sense is always already self-serving" (59). In turning to the theory of evolution, Wilson repeats the common confusion between the survival of genetic material and the pursuit of individual self-interest.[58] Since he wants to argue that all thought is guided by the drive for self-preservation, he posits that thinking is inherently narcissistic. In contrast, Freud insists that humans often engage in self-destructive behavior, and our ability to reject reality on a mental level means that we are not strictly guided by natural selection or self-preservation.[59]

As I have been arguing throughout this book, when one misunderstands the basic concepts of psychoanalysis, one is unable to maintain an effective analytic position in the clinic. This relation between theory and practice is evident in the following passage: "Most often, though, if the analyst is "thinking theory" in a clinical hour, she is likely using it as a way to maintain a feeling of independence from difficult internal experiences of whatever valence (boredom, frustration, excitement, hatred, passion, and the like)" (61). Wilson, here, presents an inverted conception of psychoanalysis; instead of seeing theory as a way of promoting analytic neutrality, he argues that theory can serve as a resistance to the analysts thinking about their own thoughts and feelings. Yet, doesn't the working through of the transference require the analyst to suspend any judgment, including the judgments about his or her own thoughts, feelings, and reactions?[60] It appears that the radical nature of analytic neutrality is just too alienating and difficult for many analysts and therapists to accept.

Instead of seeing the analyst as representing an unknowable desire in the process of analysis, Wilson concentrates on the way the analyst seeks to satisfy his or her own desire when working with patients: "The analyst is always, in part, looking for lost objects, trying to refind herself in the patient and to see herself as an analyst in day-to-day clinical work. The crucial question is how these desires facilitate or hinder a successful analytic process" (61). This notion that the analyst is looking for his or her own lost past objects represents a major deviation from analytic practice and theory since the neutrality of the analyst requires a suspension of this self-interest as one takes on the position of being an impersonal, empty mirror.[61] We can, thus consider counter-transference as anything that prevents the analyst from taking on this position.

As Wilson appears to understand, when the analyst pursues personal interests, values, and desires, the patient will react with resistances:

> resistance is fundamentally an intersubjective phenomenon. The analyst's desire—as it is expressed through specific wishes and demands—engenders resistance when the patient feels forced to recognize it. Especially during moments of uncertainty or uncomfortable silence or interaction—in which the analyst feels in her bones caught in an enactment with a patient—the analyst is tempted to fall back for defensive purposes on certain cherished identifications with a theory, a supervisor, a colleague, or her analyst. Precisely when we feel lost we want to refind ourselves. Here we are in the by now familiar place of the exercising of judgment under uncertain conditions: bias looms larger in these moments. (62)

This accurate description of counter-transference and the resistance it generates fails to provide an escape from this imaginary dualistic conflict between the ego and the other.[62] The way that the analyst exists from this dynamic is by refusing to be the one who knows, recognizes, and cares. As soon as the analyst takes on the position of the Other in the idealizing or mirroring transference, the only thing that one can do is placate the unconscious demands of the patient or frustrate the demands and produce resistance.[63] As Lacan insists, the key move is to suspend this imaginary relation by remaining neutral.

At times, Wilson does recognize the importance of theory in helping to guide the analyst's technique, but at the other times, he represents theory as a way of hiding the analyst's desire: "The analyst is in a more difficult spot, however, if she cloaks her desire in a theory of technique that she assumes to be true and takes for granted, thereby naturalizing her desire by way of that theory" (66). The problem with this formulation is that it is difficult to imagine how an analyst would not be guided by a theory considered to be true unless no theory at all was being used. In opposition to Wilson's argument, I have posited that psychoanalytic theory is necessary in order to prevent the analyst from operating on the level of imaginary identification, rivalry, recognition, and understanding.[64] In fact, Wilson himself makes this point in turning to Lacan's theory of imaginary narcissism: "The dual-relation resistance is, as we have seen, a dyadically constructed 'field of contest' (as Lacan wrote in his Mirror Stage paper): it is either you or me, my desire or yours. There is no breathing room in such a situation, no third term or point of reference that both parties can look to or use to gain perspective on the interaction" (66). In his early works, Lacan claims that by taking on the position of the symbolic Other, the analyst can help to form a social pact with the patient that moves beyond imaginary rivalry.[65] However, he later argues that this promotion of the social third-party only reinforces the transference, and so it is necessary for the analyst to take a position embodied by an object outside of the symbolic order.[66] From a theoretical perspective, analytic neutrality stands outside of the imaginary, the symbolic, and the real—the analyst is an artificial construction representing the limits of language, imagination, and reality itself.[67]

The outside status of the analytic position is described by Wilson in the following manner: "In order for a reliably valid causal relation to be established an independent variable is needed. In psychoanalysis, it is ethically incumbent upon the analyst to find a way to remove herself from the field of contest" (66). Of course, it is difficult for people to take on this position because they are so used to playing an active role in their relationships, and yet Freud insisted that one of the biggest issues for the end of analysis was the ability of people to take a passive position because it implies castration.[68] In other words, the analyst has to accept a castrated role so that neutrality becomes possible.

The Resistance of Narcissism

Like so many other therapists and analysts, Wilson has a difficult time maintaining his neutrality because he wants to help his patients by interpreting their defenses:

> Generally speaking, my approach to his problems during this first year of analysis was to examine his conflicts with him (though Robert was often not "with me"), specifically the imagined negative consequences of various actions, should he take them. "How is it, exactly, that you know Kerrie doesn't want to go on another date?" Or, "Oh, I see. So it's easier to think you know the outcome rather than find out. What do you worry will happen?" Such were typical comments I would make to Robert, which he tended to hear not as open-minded questions but as criticisms and subtle prods to be other than he was. (67–68)

What Wilson reveals in this passage is the notion that when an analyst tries to intervene directly in a patient's psychopathology, even the most well-intentioned interpretations can be experienced as direct attacks on the subject.[69] Lacan's solution to this problem was to claim that the interpretations should always be ambiguous so that they avoid being seen as judgments or criticisms.[70] Of course, this is easier said than done, but the key is for the analyst to give up the position of being the one who knows what is the truth or what is morally right. Often, the best way to intervene is to simply ask an open question predicated on the desire to produce more unknown unconscious material.[71]

At times, Wilson does show an awareness of the need to interpret from a position of non-knowledge:

> So I pulled back, and not in a "lick my wounds" kind of way. I quite consciously decided not to interpret the defensive aspects of Robert's pseudo-nonchalance or his complaints of despair. I simply asked him to tell me more about these feelings. I let him know through a variety of questions and an openness in my tone and quality of my presence that I wanted to hear more, not less. Over the next several weeks, seemingly in direct response to this shift in my subjectivity—a shift, that is, in the objects of my analytic desire—Robert gave more full-throated expression to his

> suffering. And his way of speaking gradually came to have a different aspect. He talked about his despair without massaging it. He had moments of genuinely questioning himself without demanding immediate answers from me or condemning himself for not knowing them. (70)

By maintaining an open position, Wilson was better able to break out of the imaginary relationship with his patient; in other terms, his neutrality enabled the patient to be less judgmental about his own thoughts and feelings, which in turn, allowed more unconscious material to surface:

> In my estimation, there was no other way out of this infinite regress than for me to stop contributing to it. As I removed myself from the field of contest, Robert felt much freer to think about himself. This showed in his ability, perhaps for the first time in our working together, to analyze himself. As he talked about the details of how bad he felt at times, he began to notice he was feeling better. He became more curious about his own thoughts and spoke more freely. He felt more "in control" and less overwhelmed. In short, instead of his feeling that I was implicitly telling him what to do and how to be—forms of ignoring him, as he felt his parents had done repeatedly— he now felt that I did, really and in fact, want to listen to how he was feeling. (70–71)

We see here why Lacan argued that every analytic treatment is a training analysis since what the patient has to learn is how to analyze himself or herself by taking on the position of non-judgmental neutrality.[72] We also grasp the reason why analysts have to undergo their own analysis so that they can learn the value of suspending judgment through their own personal experience.

Notes

1. Wilson, Mitchell. *The Analyst's Desire: The Ethical Foundation of Clinical Practice*. Bloomsbury Publishing USA, 2020.
2. Thompson, M. Guy. *The ethic of honesty: The fundamental rule of psychoanalysis*. Vol. 2. Rodopi, 2004.
3. Thompson, M, Guy. "The rule of neutrality." *Psychoanalysis and Contemporary Thought* 19.1 (1996): 57–84.

4. Corveleyn, Jozef. "In Defense of Benevolent Neutrality: Against a" Spiritual Strategy"." *Individual Psychology* 56.3 (2000): 343.
5. Lacan, Jacques, Alan Sheridan, and Malcolm Bowie. "The Direction of the Treatment and the Principles of its Power 1." *Écrits*. Routledge, 2020. 250–310.
6. Hoffer, Axel, and Virginia R. Youngren. "Is free association still at the core of psychoanalysis?." *The International Journal of Psychoanalysis* 85.6 (2004): 1489–1492.
7. Lothane, Zvi. "Reciprocal free association: Listening with the third ear as an instrument in psychoanalysis." *Psychoanalytic Psychology* 23.4 (2006): 711.
8. Thompson, M, Guy. "The ethics of psychoanalysis: An introduction." *Psychoanalytic review* 86.4 (1999): 503–512.
9. Shane, Morton, and Estelle Shane. "Chapter 3 Self Psychology in Search of the Optimal: A Consideration of Optimal Responsiveness, Optimal Provision, Optimal Gratif." *Progress in Self Psychology* 12 (1996): 37–54.
10. Meissner, W. W. "The problem of self-disclosure in psychoanalysis." *Journal of the American Psychoanalytic Association* 50.3 (2002): 827–867.
11. Fink, Bruce. "Against understanding: Why understanding should not be viewed as an essential aim of psychoanalytic treatment." *Journal of the American Psychoanalytic Association* 58.2 (2010): 259–285.
12. Colman, Warren. "Is the Analyst A Good Object?." *British Journal of Psychotherapy* 22.3 (2006): 295–310.
13. Fink, Bruce. *Lacan on love: An exploration of Lacan's seminar VIII, transference*. John Wiley & Sons, 2017.
14. Malin, Barnet D. "Kohut and Lacan: mirror opposites." *Psychoanalytic Inquiry* 31.1 (2011): 58–74.
15. Lacan, Jacques, Alan Sheridan, and Malcolm Bowie. "The Direction of the Treatment and the Principles of its Power 1." *Écrits*. Routledge, 2020. 250–310.
16. Chetrit-Vatine, Viviane. *The ethical seduction of the analytic situation: The feminine-maternal origins of responsibility for the other*. Routledge, 2018.
17. Benjamin, Jessica. *The bonds of love: Psychoanalysis, feminism, and the problem of domincation*. Pantheon, 2013.
18. Freud, Sigmund. "The dynamics of transference." *The standard edition of the complete psychological works of Sigmund Freud, Volume XII (1911-1913): The case of Schreber, papers on technique and other works.* 1958. 97–108.

19. Samuels, Robert. "Ethos, Transference, and Liberal Cynicism." *Zizek and the Rhetorical Unconscious*. Palgrave Macmillan, Cham, 2020. 49–63.
20. Buhle, Mari Jo, and Mari Jo Buhle. *Feminism and its discontents: A century of struggle with psychoanalysis*. Harvard University Press, 2009.
21. Gentile, Jill, and Michael Macrone. *Feminine law: Freud, free speech, and the voice of desire*. Routledge, 2018.
22. Felman, Shoshana. "Psychoanalysis and education: Teaching terminable and interminable." *Yale French Studies* 63 (1982): 21–44.
23. Freud, Sigmund. *The question of lay analysis: Conversations with an impartial person*. WW Norton & Company, 1969.
24. Freud, Sigmund, and J. Strachey. "Observations on transference-love (further recommendations on the technique of psycho-analysis III)." (1915): 157–171.
25. Hamburg, Paul. "Interpretation and empathy: reading Lacan with Kohut." *International journal of psycho-analysis* 72 (1991): 347–361.
26. Dervin, Daniel. "Where Freud was, there Lacan shall be: Lacan and the fate of transference." *American Imago* 54.4 (1997): 347–375.
27. Samuels, Robert. "Transference and Narcissism." *Freud for the Twenty-First Century*. Palgrave Pivot, Cham, 2019. 43–51.
28. Lacan, Jacques, Alan Sheridan, and Malcolm Bowie. "Aggressivity in psychoanalysis." *Ecrits*. Routledge, 2020. 9–32.
29. Lacan, Jacques. *The Ego in Freud's Theory and in the Technique of Psychoanalysis, 1954-1955*. Vol. 2. WW Norton & Company, 1991.
30. Felman, Shoshana. *Jacques Lacan and the adventure of insight: Psychoanalysis in contemporary culture*. Harvard University Press, 1987.
31. Fink, Bruce. *A clinical introduction to Lacanian psychoanalysis: Theory and technique*. Harvard University Press, 1999.
32. Libbrecht, Katrien. "The original sin of psychoanalysis: On the desire of the analyst." *Key concepts of Lacanian psychoanalysis*. Routledge, 2018. 75–100.
33. Cauwe, Joachim, Stijn Vanheule, and Mattias Desmet. "The presence of the analyst in Lacanian treatment." *Journal of the American Psychoanalytic Association* 65.4 (2017): 609–638.
34. Harari, Roberto. *Lacan's four fundamental concepts of psychoanalysis: An introduction*. Other Press, LLC, 2004.
35. Wolf, Bogdan. *Anxiety Between Desire and the Body: What Lacan Says in Seminar X*. Routledge, 2019.

36. Miller, Jacques-Alain. "How Psychoanalysis Cures According to Lacan The First Paris/Chicago Psychoanalytic Workshop, 1986 I My title is meant as a tribute to Heinz Kohut's last work, How Psychoanalysis Cures. As to Lacan, I suppose there are both people." *Newsletter of the Freudian Field* 1.2 (1987).
37. Berkenkotter, Carol. *Patient tales: Case histories and the uses of narrative in psychiatry*. Univ of South Carolina Press, 2008.
38. Rosner, Stanley. "On the nature of free association." *Journal of the American Psychoanalytic Association* 21.3 (1973): 558–575.
39. Spence, Donald P. *Narrative truth and historical truth: Meaning and interpretation in psychoanalysis*. WW Norton & Company, 1984.
40. Freud, Sigmund. "Recommendations to physicians practising psycho-analysis." *London: The* (1912).
41. Aron, Lewis. "From hypnotic suggestion to free association: Freud as a psychotherapist, circa 1892–1893." *Contemporary Psychoanalysis* 32.1 (1996): 99–114.
42. Muller, John, P. "Ego and subject in Lacan." *Psychoanalytic review* 69.2 (1982): 234–240.
43. Lacan, Jacques. "Some reflections on the ego 1." *Influential Papers from the 1950s*. Routledge, 2018. 292–306.
44. Apollon, Willy, Danielle Bergeron, and Lucie Cantin. *After Lacan: Clinical practice and the subject of the unconscious*. SUNY Press, 2002.
45. Samuels, Robert. "Logos, global justice, and the reality principle." *Zizek and the rhetorical unconscious*. Palgrave Macmillan, Cham, 2020. 65–86.
46. Samuels, Robert. "Science and the reality principle." *Freud for the twenty-first century*. Palgrave Pivot, Cham, 2019. 5–16.
47. Mills, Jon. "Lacan on paranoiac knowledge." *Psychoanalytic Psychology* 20.1 (2003): 30.
48. Goldberg, Arnold. "The tension between realism and relativism in psychoanalysis." *Psychoanalysis and contemporary thought*7.3 (1984): 367–386.
49. Samuels, Robert. *The Psychopathology of Political Ideologies*. Routledge, 2021.
50. Khoury, Maurice. "The desire of the analyst and counter-transference: from the mirroring analyst to the desiring analyst." *The Lacan Tradition*. Routledge, 2018. 189–206.
51. Fink, Bruce. "5. The Subject and the Other's Desire." *The Lacanian Subject*. Princeton University Press, 2017. 49–68.

52. Samuels, Robert. "Science and the reality principle." *Freud for the twenty-first century*. Palgrave Pivot, Cham, 2019. 5–16.
53. Freud, Sigmund. "Negation." *Organization and pathology of thought: Selected sources*. Columbia University Press, 1951. 338–348.
54. Kerrigan, William. "Psychoanalysis and the Vicissitudes of Enlightenment." *American Imago* 48.2 (1991): 265–278.
55. Lacan, Jacques. "Some reflections on the ego." *International Journal of Psycho-Analysis* 34 (1953): 11–17.
56. Boothby, Richard. *Freud as philosopher: Metapsychology after Lacan*. Routledge, 2015.
57. Hole, Richard W., Augustus J. Rush, and Aaron T. Beck. "A cognitive investigation of schizophrenic delusions." *Psychiatry*42.4 (1979): 312–319.
58. Samuels, Robert. "Damasio's Error: The Politics of Biological Determinism After Freud." *Psychoanalyzing the Politics of the New Brain Sciences*. Palgrave Pivot, Cham, 2017. 9–33.
59. Poeldinger, W. J. "The psychopathology and psychodynamics of self-destruction." *Crisis: The Journal of Crisis Intervention and Suicide Prevention* (1989).
60. Palomera, Vicente. "Modalities of the Transference." *Analysis*5 (1994): 17–26.
61. Reed, Gail S. "An empty mirror: reflections on nonrepresentation." *The Psychoanalytic Quarterly* 78.1 (2009): 1–26.
62. Van Pelt, Tamise. "Otherness." *Postmodern Culture* 10.2 (2000).
63. Lacan, Jacques, Alan Sheridan, and Malcolm Bowie. "The Direction of the Treatment and the Principles of its Power 1." *Écrits*. Routledge, 2020. 250–310.
64. Nobus, Dany. *Jacques Lacan and the Freudian practice of psychoanalysis*. Routledge, 2013.
65. Miller, Jacques-Alain, ed. *The Seminar of Jacques Lacan: Book 1: Freud's Papers on Technique 1953-1954*. CUP Archive, 1988.
66. Vanier, Alain. *Lacan*. Other Press, LLC, 2020.
67. Samuels, Robert. *Between philosophy and psychoanalysis: Lacan's reconstruction of Freud*. Routledge, 2014.
68. Freud, Sigmund. "Analysis Terminable and Interminable." *The International Journal of Psycho-Analysis* 18 (1937): 373.
69. Siebers, Tobin. "7. The Ethical Unconscious: From Freud to Lacan." *The Ethics of Criticism*. Cornell University Press, 2018. 159–185.

70. Stevens, Alexandre. "Lacanian interpretation." *Hurly-Burly: The International Lacanian Journal of Psychoanalysis* 1 (2009): 57–59.
71. Fink, Bruce. *A clinical introduction to Lacanian psychoanalysis: Theory and technique*. Harvard University Press, 1999.
72. Hammill, Graham. "Being and knowledge: Lacan and the institution of psychoanalysis." *The American Journal of Semiotics* 15.1/4 (2008): 137–167.

6

Zizek and the Empty Unconscious

This chapter argues that the work of Slavoj Zizek has been one of the major causes for the contemporary misunderstanding of psychoanalysis. Through a close reading of his first major book, *The Sublime Object of Ideology*, I will explore how he distorts the meaning of the unconscious, primary processes, the pleasure principle, the reality principle, and transference.[1] I will also examine the possibility of using psychoanalytic treatment on a social and cultural level. The key question here is how do we work through the fundamental fantasies shaping our relationship to others?

From Freud to Lacan

From a psychoanalytic perspective, the central conflict shaping every society and individual is the relationship between the moral conscience (the super-ego) and individual drives (the pleasure principle).[2] For Freud, this conflict is ultimately unresolvable, and so there can be no perfect relation between the self and others.[3] In fact, a major goal of analysis is to help people to see that the pursuit of pleasure and the

R. Samuels, *(Mis)Understanding Freud with Lacan, Zizek, and Neuroscience*, The Palgrave Lacan Series, https://doi.org/10.1007/978-3-031-13327-5_6

demands of social organization (civilization) will always be in conflict with each other.[4] Moreover, it is often personal and ideological fantasies that seek to resolve this antinomy on an imaginary level.[5] Psychoanalytic treatment then is primarily focused on working through these distorting thought-structures.[6]

Doubling the divide between the social and the individual, we find the opposition of language and reality. Since, we can never fully present the real through symbolic representations, our knowledge is always limited.[7] It is therefore important to affirm that language alienates us from reality and that the truth is never complete or whole.[8] While it is true that the only medium of psychoanalysis is speech, it is vital to realize that speech is based on a system of associations, substitutions, and displacements.[9] The goal of analysis, then, should not be the complete symbolic narrative of a person's life or the attainment of some comprehensive knowledge; rather, one has to realize the different ways reality has been misrepresented through imaginary mental productions while at the same time seeking to attain the necessary but impossible ideal of knowing the truth of one's inner and outer life.[10] Thus, the desire of the analyst and the desire of the patient are identical: They desire to discover the truth, but since they can never know the whole truth, they continue to desire to know more.[11] In fact, if we follow Lacan in affirming that desire is always directed towards something one does not have, it must be impossible for desire to be ever satisfied.[12]

In the case of Zizek's use of Lacan's work, this question of desire is presented near the start of *The Sublime Object of Ideology*:

> The famous Lacanian motto not to give way on one's desire (ne pas cider sur son desir) - is aimed at the fact that we must not obliterate the distance separating the Real from its symbolization: it is this surplus of the Real over every symbolization that functions as the object-cause of desire. To come to terms with this surplus (or, more. precisely, leftover) means to acknowledge a fundamental deadlock ('antagonism'), a kernel resisting symbolic integration-dissolution. (xxv)

On the hand, Zizek recognizes here the opposition between the social symbolic and the real, but then on the other hand, he quickly privileges the real instead of stressing the psychoanalytic focus on the conflict between the two. As we shall see, this focus on the unknowable real tends to dominate his work and his views of the goals of psychoanalysis.[13] In fact, I will argue that there is an underlying libertarian fantasy driving his discourse, which centers on the idealization of the pleasure principle over the social super-ego.[14]

Following the teachings of Jacques-Alain Miller, Zizek believes that the "Early Lacan" stressed the role of language and the social Other, while the "Late Lacan," emphasized the role played by enjoyment (jouissance), the real, and the death drive.[15] Underlying this reading is the unconscious fantasy of the subject who is free to enjoy in opposition to the castrating and censoring social order. In other words, instead of positing the fundamental conflict between the symbolic social super-ego and individual enjoyment, Miller and Zizek tend to privilege the real over the symbolic and the individual over the social.[16]

Coupled with his own pronouncements that "the Other does not exist" and "there is no such thing as a sexual relation," Lacan's focus on what he calls jouissance (orgasm, pleasure, release) shapes the last stage of his teachings, and so there is a good reason for Miller's and Zizek's misunderstandings of psychoanalysis.[17] Moreover, Lacan, in his earlier teachings and writings did emphasize how the goal of analysis is to get the patient to use speech to fully integrate their own history, and this view of analytic treatment pushed him to stress the roles played by language, social order, and cultural discourse.[18] However, throughout his work, Lacan also insisted that the tragic dimension of being human revolves around the fundamental conflict between the socio-symbolic order and the resistant enjoyment of individuals, which is a restating of Freud's foundational notion of how civilization leads to discontent.[19]

The Death Drive Distortion

While Freud affirmed that society will always be at odds with the individual, he also highlighted how individuals are at odds with themselves.[20] Not only is the unconscious based on the fact that people lie to themselves, and thus they divide themselves between the truth and the lie, but the pursuit of individual pleasure is itself in conflict internally. Since the goal of the pleasure principle is to release all physical and mental tension, the generation of stimulation has to be coupled with its erasure.[21] In fact, Lacan's use of the term "jouissance" itself points to the role of release and self-consumption in sexuality by highlighting the function of an orgasm.[22] However, due to the fact that Zizek and others translate jouissance by enjoyment, they lose this aspect of release that is evident for French speakers.[23]

Since Freud highlights how pleasure concerns avoiding and releasing tension, he is able to posit a fundamental law of inertia, which he will later call the death drive.[24] If it seems absurd to equate the pursuit of pleasure with death, one only has to think of the destructive nature of addictions where one seeks out enjoyment but can end up pursuing self-destruction.[25] Likewise, when Freud in *Beyond the Pleasure Principle* describes a game he saw his grandson playing, what he stresses is that not only did this form of play represent the child using language and a symbolic object to overcome the absence of his parents, but this child also used this activity to try to make his own self-image appear and disappear in the mirror.[26] We learn from this example of the death drive that pleasure can be derived from self-effacement and the replacement of others. Like the release of stimulation through an orgasm, symbolic play can help us to escape from our own selves and our dependency on others.

Although enjoyment and the death drive are key concepts for Zizek, we shall see in the following passage how he distorts the meaning of these terms:

> Let us take the Freudian notion of the 'death drive'. of course, we have to abstract Freud's biologism: 'death drive' is not a biological fact but a notion indicating that the human psychic apparatus is subordinated to a blind automatism of repetition beyond pleasure-seeking, self-preservation, accordance between man and his milieu. Man is - Hegel dixit- 'an animal sick unto death', an animal extorted by an insatiable parasite (reason, logos, language). In this perspective, the 'death drive', this dimension of radical negativity, cannot be reduced to an expression of alienated social conditions, it defines la condition humaine as such: there is no solution, no escape from it. (xxvii)

At first glance, Zizek's interpretation of the death drive does appear to match Freud's theory concerning the relation between pleasure and release: as a compulsion to negate the self and the other through symbolic repetition, the death drive represents a break with biology and social alienation. However, it is misleading to posit that this drive defines the human condition because one still has to deal with the fundamental conflict between society and the individual.[27]

It is vital to highlight how from a psychoanalytic perspective, social order is produced and maintained through the regulation of sex and violence.[28] Furthermore, the super-ego represents the internalization of this regulation, which requires every individual to sacrifice their own drives for the benefit of the collective.[29] When Zizek insists that it is the internal death drive in the individual that determines the fundamental conflict of the human condition, he represses the role that society plays in structuring desire and division. What would be more accurate is to say that the drive to escape all tension often matches the social need to regulate sex and violence. What is very misleading is to blame the entire problem on the compulsive repetitions of the death drive in the isolated individual.

Defining Culture

Not only are we internally divided by our self-destructive urges, but we are alienated by the social order, which requires us to sacrifice our individual impulses.[30] Zizek posits that one way that these conflicts are overcome on an imaginary level is through cultural formations:

> All 'culture' is in a way a reaction-formation, an attempt to limit, canalize--to cultivate this imbalance, this traumatic kernel, this radical antagonism through which man cuts his umbilical cord with nature, with animal homeostasis. It is not only that the aim is no longer to abolish this drive antagonism, but the aspiration to abolish it is precisely the source of totalitarian temptation: the greatest mass murders and holocausts have always been perpetrated in the name of man as harmonious being, of a New Man without antagonistic tension. (xxviii)

Zizek's important insight here that cultures are often shaped by a utopian idea to eliminate fundamental conflicts leaves open the question of which conflict is fundamental. He appears to be arguing that we turn to culture in order to resolve the tension caused by the death drive and the pleasure principle. However, Freud's idea is that we first turn to imagination in the form of hallucinations in order to satisfy our unmet needs, and then when this does not work, we turn to others to help us to satisfy our needs.[31] In fact, Freud bases his theory of transference and the social link on this primary demand for caregivers to satisfy the subject's pleasure principle. As he argues in his *Project for a Scientific Psychology*, morality and communication have their roots in a primary relation where the helpless infant cries, and the parents recognize and understand this cry as a demand for a certain satisfaction. The cry is then turned into a demand through the recognition of the social Other.[32] From this moment on, when the subject asks for something, there is an underlying desire for the Other's love, knowledge, and recognition. Culture then can be understood as the way a society mystifies these relationships by combining the primary processes of imaginary satisfaction with the requirements of the social order. Ideological fantasies should therefore be seen as hiding the fundamental conflict between society and the individual through a solution that occurs purely on the level of thought.[33]

We can understand the role of culture as an ideological fantasy by examining Zizek's own discourse. In focusing on the death drive, enjoyment, and the inexistence of the social Other, he resolves the conflict between the social and the individual by indirectly privileging the libertarian subject of freedom and compulsive pleasure.[34] While I do not think that Zizek would approve of this interpretation, this repressed ideological fantasy continues to return throughout his work. Moreover, one reason for this symptomatic repetition is that he conflates the five levels of conflict shaping psychoanalysis and human subjectivity: (1) the conflict between stimulation and release (the pleasure principle); (2) the conflict between reality and imaginative thought (the primary processes); (3) the conflict between society and the individual (transference); (4) the conflict between the ego and the super-ego (the unconscious); and (5) the conflict between the Symbolic and the Real (the reality principle). We should therefore think of the misunderstanding of psychoanalysis as generated from the refusal to accept these foundational antinomies.

From Lacan to Marx and Back Again

If Zizek's work can be considered to be an ideological fantasy, then we need to see how he constructs this imaginary reconciliation in his text. One of the main ways he unifies opposing forces is through his attempt to reconcile psychoanalysis with Marxism:[35]

> According to Lacan, it was none other than Karl Marx who invented the notion of symptom. Is this Lacanian thesis just a sally of wit, a vague analogy, or does it possess a pertinent theoretical foundation? If Marx really articulated the notion of the symptom as it is also at work in the Freudian field, then we must ask ourselves the Kantian question, concerning the epistemological 'conditions of possibility' of such an encounter: how was it possible for Marx, in his analysis of the world of commodities, to produce a notion which applies also to the analysis of dreams, hysterical phenomena, and so on? (3)

This combination of Lacan and Marx replicates a common Western academic desire to reconcile theories based on society with theories centered on the individual.[36] In Zizek's case, he attempts to equate Marx's economic theory of commodity exchange with Freud's notions of symptoms, dreams, and hysteria.

The way that Zizek brings together Marxism and psychoanalysis is by highlighting how in both discourses, the emphasis of interpretation is on form and not content:[37]

> The answer is that there is a fundamental homology between the interpretative procedure of Marx and Freud - more precisely, between their analysis of commodity and of dreams. In both cases the point is to avoid the properly fetishistic fascination of the 'content' supposedly hidden behind the form: the 'secret' to be unveiled through analysis is not the content hidden by the form (the form of commodities, the form of dreams) but, on the contrary, the secret of this form itself. The theoretical intelligence of the form of dreams does not consist in penetrating from the manifest content to its 'hidden kernel', to the latent dream-thoughts; it consists in the answer to the question: why have the latent dream-thoughts assumed such a form, why were they transposed into the form of a dream? (3)

In this privileging of form over content, Zizek makes the important move of eliminating both social and subjective material from the consideration of capitalism and subjectivity.[38] Thus, instead of looking at the content of a dream or the material derived from free association, Zizek's formalism removes signification and individual experience from psychoanalysis and Marxism. This emptying out of content to focus on form is odd for someone who is known for his insightful political and cultural interpretations.[39]

One possible explanation for Zizek's formalism is his understanding of the key psychoanalytic concept of the unconscious:

> But as Freud continually emphasizes, there is nothing 'unconscious' in the 'latent dream thought: this thought is an entirely 'normal' thought which can be articulated in the syntax of everyday, common language; topologically, it belongs to the system of, consciousness/preconsciousness'; the subject is usually aware of it, even excessively so; it harasses him all the time … Under certain conditions this thought is pushed away, forced out of the consciousness, drawn into the unconscious - that is, submitted to the laws of the 'primary process', translated into the 'language of the unconscious'. (4)

Once again, at first glance, this interpretation of unconscious thoughts seems correct, but there are two major issues: one is the relation between this passage and Zizek's formalism, and the other concerns the relationship between the unconscious and the primary processes.

In terms of the formal nature of the unconscious, what is lost in this approach is the question of why the subject seeks to avoid these thoughts in the first place. According to Freud's theory of repression, the neurotic subject desires to escape feelings of guilt, shame, and fear by replacing these thoughts and feelings with other representations.[40] It is essential for psychoanalytic treatment to reveal these repressed thoughts through speech, and so the content is more important than the form. In removing the content from consideration, the process then becomes a practice in empty formalism, and we shall see that this formalism points to Zizek's tendency to promote a type of behaviorism where subjectivity is put in a black box as the focus is placed on externalized practices.[41]

It is also necessary to point out that the formal aspects of the primary processes—substitution, displacement, association, and projection—do reshape unconscious thoughts, but these thoughts themselves are derived from the fundamental conflict between the individual and the social.[42] Since one represses feelings of guilt and shame, and these feelings are derived from the internalization of social norms and morality, the internal conflict between the super-ego and the ideal ego replicates the larger conflict between the self and society.[43] When one concentrates on the form and not the content of this conflict, one loses the important distinction between the unconscious thoughts and the forms of the primary processes.

Zizek's misunderstanding of the unconscious is apparent in the following passage where he rejects some of the core aspects of unconscious content:

> if we seek the 'secret of the dream' in the latent content hidden by the manifest text, we are doomed to disappointment: all we find is some entirely 'normal' – albeit usually unpleasant - thought, the nature of which is mostly non-sexual and definitely not 'unconscious'. This 'normal', conscious/preconscious thought is not drawn towards the unconscious, repressed simply because of its 'disagreeable' character for the conscious, but because it achieves a kind of 'short circuit' between it and another desire which is already repressed, located in the unconscious, a desire which has nothing whatsoever to do with the latent dream-thought. (5)

Although Zizek wants to disconnect the unconscious from strictly unpleasant thoughts, the Freudian unconscious is founded on the repression of anything that undermines the ego's sense of moral righteousness or personal competence. Moreover, while the obsessional subject may engage in acts of purification to keep impure thoughts out of mind, these feelings of guilt and shame remain in the unconscious where they are reworked by the primary processes.[44] Likewise, in the case of hysteria, the repression of sexual fixations and fantasies results in a return of repressed impulses coupled with a defense against them in a contradictory formation.[45] In both cases, analytic treatment works by discovering this repressed material through the process of free association and the working through of the transference; it therefore makes no sense to argue that only the form of the primary processes is important.

Exchange Value

One reason why Zizek may seek to eliminate the content of the unconscious is that he wants to show that behind modern science and democracy, one finds the formal nihilism of capitalist exchange value: "Before thought could arrive at the idea of a purely quantitative determination, a sine qua non of the modern science of nature, pure quantity was already at work in money, that commodity which renders possible the commensurability of the value of all other commodities not withstanding their particular qualitative determination" (11). The theory here is that underlying the modern scientific practice of analyzing nature through the use of abstract symbols and concepts, we find the abstract quantification caused by the capitalist exchange value.[46] Since any object or act of labor can be represented by a shared symbolic mediation (money), all other values and meanings are eliminated.[47] Thus, when Marx posits that in modern capitalism, all past feudal values and relations melt away, he was pointing to the way exchange value replaces every other value.

It is interesting to note that this nihilism of capitalism dovetails with Zizek's own method of emptying out the meaning of key psychoanalytic concepts: by insisting on form over content, Zizek melts away all of the meaning and value of Freud's original theories. We see this move to a universalized nihilism in his combination of Marx and Hegel:

> That is to say, if we look closely at the ontological status of what Sohn-Rethel calls the 'real abstraction' [das reale Abstraktion (that is, the act of abstraction at work in the very active process of the exchange of commodities), the homology between its status and that of the unconscious, this signifying chain which persists on 'another Scene', is striking: the 'real abstraction ' is the unconscious of the transcendental subject, the support of objective-universal scientific knowledge. (11)

This combination of Hegel's real abstraction, Marx's exchange value, and Lacan's theory of the unconscious reveals the way that Zizek is able to jump from one discourse to the other because he empties out the meaning of each one.[48] As Jean Baudrillard argues, what in part defines contemporary culture is the lost distinction among different discourses, which is itself the result of the combination of capitalism with science and art and the lack of any cultural filtering system.[49] Zizek's own discourse then reflects this aspect of contemporary post-postmodern culture. Not only does he jump from high culture to low culture, but he also has no problem moving from Hegel to Marx to Lacan. In fact, *The Sublime Object of Ideology* represents the foundation of the main arguments he will make in his later books, and we can thus read the entirety of his work through an analysis of this early text.

On one level, he is correct to highlight how the formal primary processes of association, substitution, and displacement function in part by eliminating natural (time) and social differences (categories), but on the other hand, he confuses this automatic mental symbolism with the meaning-destroying force of exchange value. In other words, it is true that in our dreams, we treat things like words and words like things, but this type of fetishism is different from the fetishism caused by the generalized mediation of symbolic currencies.[50] The latter type of fetishism is much closer to the symbolic dimension of the death drive, which is centered on the way drives function through the substitution of objects and the re-iteration of symbolic social differences (idealized vs. debased, active vs. passive, Madonna vs. whore, affection vs. desire).[51]

Cynical Behaviorism

The clearest example of Zizek's formalism can be seen in his focus on social practices shaped by exchange value:

> we know very well that money, like all other material objects, suffers the effects of use, that its material body changes through time, but in the social activity of the market we none the less treat coins as if they consist 'of an immutable substance, a substance over which time has no power, and which stands in antithetic contrast to any matter found in nature' How tempting to recall here the formula of fetishistic disavowal: 'I know very well, but still … '. To the current exemplifications of this formula ('I know that Mother has not got a phallus, but still … [I believe she has got one]; 'I know that Jews are people like us, but still … [there is something in them,)

> we must undoubtedly add also the variant of money: 'I know that money is a material object like others, but still … [it is as if it were made of a special substance over which time has no power)'. (12)

In this structure of fetishistic disavowal, the subject is split between the perception of reality and a symbolic substitution that is treated as the real thing.[52] Thus, in Freud's classic example, the male child sees that the mother does not have a penis, but he acts as if she still has the universal symbol of sexual identity. In fact, according to Freud's theory, the fetishist will fixate on an object (a shoe, hair, clothing) that was seen right before the discovery of the missing phallus. As a form of exchange value, the imaginary phallus or fetish represents a substitution of the primary lost object.[53]

We can say with Zizek that the sexual drive and the economic exchange value share the same structure—both rely on symbolic substitution. However, Zizek extends this analogy by including a whole range of social beliefs and ideological practices centered on idealization and the sublime:

> Here we have touched a problem unsolved by Marx, that of the material character of money: not of the empirical, material stuff money is made of, but of the sublime material, of that other 'indestructible and immutable' body which persists beyond the corruption of the body physical – this other body of money is like the corpse of the Sadeian victim which endures all torments and survives with its beauty immaculate. This immaterial corporality of the 'body within the body' gives us a precise definition of the sublime object, and it is in this sense only that the psychoanalytic notion of money as a 'pre-phallic', 'anal' object is acceptable – provided that we do not forget how this postulated existence of the sublime body depends on the symbolic order: the indestructible 'body-within-the-body' exempted from the effects of wear and tear is always sustained by the guarantee of some symbolic authority. (12–13)

Similar to Lacan's notion of the sublime love object in Courtly Love, the idealized cause of desire embodies a symbolic social value, yet this object-choice is in direct opposition to the object of the drive.[54] As Lacan insists, when lovers describe their beloved in this tradition, it always sounds like they are describing the same person, and that is because the object is not a real person but a symbolic cultural ideal. Moreover, Freud insists that in the hypnotic love relation, the lover becomes humble and humiliated as the ego-ideal is followed with blind obedience.[55]

It is crucial to contrast the masochistic submission to the idealized object with the object of the exchange value since it is precisely capitalism that undermines the feudal discourse of idealization.[56] From a historical and psychological perspective, modern capitalism allows the break from premodern religion, feudalism, and monarchy through the replacement of traditional values with the meaningless calculation of market value.[57] In terms of psychoanalysis, premodern institutions rely on the transference of responsibility from the individual to the transcendent idea, leader, or love object, while in the perverse realm of the drives, the pursuit of individual pleasure and self-interest is fueled by a debasement of the object and denial of the social Other.[58] Therefore, when Zizek equates money with the Sadean victim and the sublime object of desire, he is conflating the foundation of transference with the pleasure principle.

I have been stressing that is vital to separate the key concepts of transference, the pleasure principle, the primary processes, and the unconscious because without these differences, one loses the specificity of psychoanalysis itself. The risk of Zizek's work, then, is that he tends to empty the meaning out of these concepts so that he can combine together different discourses in a unified perspective.[59] For instance, the following passage attempts to equate Marxism and psychoanalysis by conflating economic exchange value with the unconscious and the primary processes:

> "The exchange abstraction is not thought, but it has the form of thought." Here we have one of the possible definitions of the unconscious: the form of thought whose ontological status is not that of thought, that is to say, the form of thought external to the thought itself - in short, some Other Scene external to the thought whereby the form of the thought is already articulated in advance. The symbolic order is precisely such a formal order which supplements and/or disrupts the dual relationship of 'external' factual reality and 'internal' subjective experience. (13)

As Zizek moves from exchange value to thought to the unconscious to the symbolic order, he is once again confusing four different modes of symbolism. On one level, we have the symbolic substitution of objects and values through the capitalistic market value system.[60] I have equated this form of symbolic activity to the drives and the pleasure principle because for psychoanalysis, every object of desire is a substitute for an original object that is always already lost—the mother.[61] This mode of symbolic substitution is distinct from the way that the primary processes shape thinking through association, substitution, and displacement. Thus, the representations in dreams are always symbols representing something else in a network of signifiers structured by symbolic substitution, association, and displacement. One of Freud's radical moves is to argue that thought itself is determined by these automatic primary processes, which treat things as words and words as things.[62]

Not only should we distinguish the symbolic nature of the primary processes from the symbolic aspects of the drives, but we also have to recognize the difference between these symbolic forms and the symbolic social order. Since societies often structure their social hierarchies through the use of symbolic oppositions (male vs. female, human vs. animal, reason vs. emotion, master vs. slave), language plays a central role in producing and maintaining social order.[63] Moreover, from a psychoanalytic perspective, one of the main questions is how does an individual become subjected to the social symbolic order? The three main answers to this question are castration, identification, and transference.[64] Freud stresses that castration as a threat of bodily harm scares people into accepting social authority structured by the social hierarchy.[65] In turn, as a way of resolving the conflict between the child and the parents (the Oedipus complex), the male child identifies with the castrater, and the female child identifies with the castrated subject.[66] The cause of castration is then idealized in the transference by allowing the subject the ability to place all responsibility into the hands of the all-powerful Other.

Of course, neurotics resist accepting both the automatic nature of the primary processes and the threat of symbolic castration, and so these aspects of subjectivity are repressed into the unconscious.[67] It is therefore necessary to counter Zizek's effort to equate symbolic thought, exchange value, social order, and the unconscious because these different levels of human subjectivity structure both the theory and practice of psychoanalysis. When we fail to differentiate these fundamental concepts, we end up with an empty formalistic behaviorism, which is evident in the following claim by Zizek: "there, in the external effectivity of the exchange process … there is the theatre in which your truth was performed before you took cognizance of it" (14). Like Skinner's behaviorism, the focus on social behavior can result in placing subjectivity in an excluded black box.[68] By saying that with the exchange value, truth is performed prior to any cognition, we lose the very essence of psychoanalysis itself. In fact, we see in Zizek's definition of ideology how he clings to a new form of behaviorism:

> the social effectivity of the exchange process is a kind of reality which is possible only on condition that the individuals partaking in it are not aware of its proper logic; that is, a kind of reality whose very ontological consistency implies a certain non-knowledge of its participants - if we come to 'know too much', to pierce the true functioning of social reality, this reality would dissolve itself. This is probably the fundamental dimension of 'ideology' … (15–16)

From this perspective, social practices and individual behaviors are effective precisely because the people engaged in these activities are not aware of what is going on.[69] For Zizek, the issue is not that we repress our desires, fears, and primary processes into the unconscious; the real issue is that the capitalist exchange value and its supporting ideology do not require subjective knowledge.[70] Zizek thus presents a psychoanalysis without content or subjectivity.

The Return of the Repressed

And yet, Zizek cannot help returning to the subjectivity of the unconscious as the repressed continues to return. One reason, then, why Zizek may be constantly re-writing the same book in an obsessional manner is that his impulse to empty every concept of its original content is coupled with his desire to be seen as providing profound insight.[71] This contradiction is apparent in his description of the interpretation of neurotic symptoms: "Thus we have finally reached the dimension of the symptom, because one of its possible definitions would also be 'a formation whose very consistency implies a certain non-knowledge on the part of the subject': the subject can 'enjoy his symptom' only in so far as its logic escapes him - the measure of the success of its interpretation is precisely its dissolution" (16). On one level, this formulation appears to match Freud's own practice of using interpretation as the cure to neurotic symptoms; however, on another level, Zizek's claim effaces analysis by devaluing the importance of the repressed material. In other terms, he highlights the lack of knowledge of the neurotic subject, but he does not examine what the neurotic subject is trying to avoid.

By emptying out the content of the unconscious and the primary processes, Zizek is able to equate the hysterical symptom with alienated social relations: "'Instead of appearing at all events as their own mutual relations, the social relations between individuals are disguised under the shape of social relations between things' - here we have a precise definition of the hysterical symptom, of the 'hysteria of conversion' proper to capitalism" (22). What enables Zizek's combination of Marxism with psychoanalysis is the replacement of subjective content with the abstract relationship between things.[72] In other words, the alienation caused by the mystification of exchange value structures Zizek's own interpretive strategy. Furthermore, his theory of cynical ideology is also shaped by this same externalized social practice:

> In the *Critique of Cynical Reason*, a great bestseller in Germany, Peter Sloterdijk puts forward the thesis that ideology's dominant mode of functioning is cynical, which renders impossible - or, more precisely, vain-the classic critical-ideological procedure. The cynical subject is quite aware of the distance between the ideological mask and the social reality, but he none the less still insists upon the mask. The formula, as proposed by Sloterdijk, would then be: 'they know very well what they are doing, but still, they are doing it'. (25)

I have been arguing that Zizek's own discourse partakes in cynical distance since he empties all terms of their original meaning and context by creating a psychoanalysis without a psychoanalytic practice.[73] In fact, we shall see that his investment in saving an idealized version of Hegel results in a reversal of Marx's own reversal of German Idealism.[74]

From Lacan to Marx to Hegel

Underlying this move from Lacan to Marx to Hegel is the promotion of a perverse borderline subjectivity where a cynical lack of belief is coupled with the exploitation of others for the gain of profit and pleasure:

> Even Adorno came to this conclusion, starting from the premise that ideology is, strictly speaking, only a system which makes a claim to the truth - that is, which is not simply a lie but a lie experienced as truth, a lie which pretends to be taken seriously. Totalitarian ideology no longer has this pretension. It is no longer meant, even by its authors, to be taken seriously - its status is just that of a means of manipulation, purely external and instrumental; its rule is secured not by its truth-value but by simple extra ideological violence and promise of gain. (27)

In emphasizing the instrumental and external foundation of totalitarian ideology, Zizek turns to a perverse and borderline mode of pathology where people are treated as things to be used and exploited.[75] From this perspective, the cynic is someone who takes advantage of a system in which he does not believe by acting on impulses and drives devoid of any coherent understanding or reason.[76] Thus, for the borderline subject, the combination of low impulse control and unstable relationships represents the privileging of the id over the social super-ego.[77] Here we see why Freud's theory of perversion matches the contemporary diagnostic category of the anti-social borderline personality disorder; through the dominance of the drives, the subject's pursuit of pleasure ultimately leads to self-destruction and the imagined freedom from the castrating social Other.[78]

In this combination of cynicism and perverse borderline subjectivity, we understand how the discourse of capitalism does rely on an unsatisfiable desire motivating a manipulation and exploitation of other people: "The problem is that in their social activity itself, in what they are doing, they are acting as if money, in its material reality, is the immediate embodiment of wealth as such. They are fetishists in practice, not in theory. What they ' do not know', what they misrecognize, is the fact that in their social reality itself, in their social activity - in the act of commodity exchange - they are guided by the fetishistic illusion" (27). By arguing that capitalists are "fetishists in practice," Zizek reveals the underlying pathology of cynical behavioral ideology: once subjectivity and unconscious content have been removed, the abstract formalism of the exchange values and the drives is able to reshape social reality.[79]

Zizek's discursive move from Lacan to Marx to Hegel results in a strange idealization of material relations: "The roots of philosophical speculative idealism are in the social reality of the world of commodities; it is this world which behaves 'idealistically'"(29). In one move, Zizek is able to empty out the meaning of both psychoanalysis and Marxism by placing subjectivity and material conditions in a black box that repeats the strategy of Skinner's behaviorism: "What they overlook, what they misrecognize, is not the reality but the illusion which is structuring their reality, their real social activity. They know very well how things really are, but still they are doing it as if they did not know. The illusion is therefore double: it consists in overlooking the illusion which is structuring our real, effective relationship to reality. And this overlooked, unconscious illusion is what may be called the ideological fantasy" (30). Since Zizek does not tie the unconscious to repression, the super-ego, and the content of the primary processes, he is able to focus on the embodiment of ideological fantasies in non-conscious behaviors.[80] It is then external reality itself which is seen as being determined by imagination.

The Displacement of Ideology

One difficulty in examining Zizek's theory of ideology is that he constantly moves from equating it with capitalism to totalitarianism to contemporary subjectivity. These displacements are made possible because each conceptual term is merely an instrument to be manipulated for the purpose of providing a counter-intuitive insight.[81] By removing the content from the concepts, ideas are able to be used freely in the same way that the behaviorist attempts to efface thoughts and feelings from the practices being conditioned. Behaviorism, consumer capitalism, libertarian politics, and perverse borderline structures share this same tendency of denying the unconscious shame and guilt associated with transgressive drives.[82] In Zizek's case, his cynical analysis of cynicism seeks to displace both psychoanalysis and Marxism: "If our concept of ideology remains the classic one in which the illusion is located in knowledge, then today's society must appear post-ideological: the prevailing ideology is that of cynicism; people no longer believe in ideological truth; they do not take ideological propositions seriously" (30). Cynical distance and behaviorism go together because in both cases, any concern for belief or truth is suspended.[83]

In fact, Zizek traces this contemporary form of cynical ideology to the transition from feudalism to modern capitalism:

> In feudalism, as we have seen, relations between people are mystified, mediated through a web of ideological beliefs and superstitions. They are the relations between the master and his servant, whereby the master exerts his charismatic power of fascination, and so forth. Although in capitalism the subjects are emancipated, perceiving themselves as free from medieval religious superstitions, when they deal with one another they do so as rational utilitarians, guided only by their selfish interests. The point of Marx' s analysis, however, is that the things (commodities) themselves believe in their place, instead of the subjects: it is as if all their beliefs, superstitions and metaphysical mystifications, supposedly surmounted by the rational, utilitarian personality, are embodied in the 'social relations between things'. (31)

This notion that things believe in the place of people believing is a great example of Freud's theory of animism, which he defines as the projection of internal mental thoughts onto external reality.[84] However, in contemporary culture, these projected thoughts are not coupled with the certainty of the psychotic subject; instead, projected ideas are experienced from a position of non-belief. Moreover, while in premodern religion and feudalism, one submits to the powerful and charismatic leader in a mode of hypnotic blind obedience, with modernity, this submission to the all-powerful father-figure is broken or driven into the unconscious.[85]

In the case of contemporary cynical ideology, Zizek posits that one no longer has to believe in beliefs since they take on a social life of their own:

> They no longer believe, but the things themselves believe for them. This seems also to be a basic Lacanian proposition, contrary to the usual thesis that a belief is something interior and knowledge something exterior (in the sense that it can be verified through an external procedure). Rather, it is belief which is radically exterior, embodied in the practical, effective procedure of people. It is similar to Tibetan prayer wheels: you write a prayer on a paper, put the rolled paper into a wheel, and turn it automatically, without thinking (or, if you want to proceed according to the Hegelian 'cunning of reason', you attach it to a windmill, so that it is moved around by the wind). In this way, the wheel itself is praying for me, instead of me - or, more precisely, I myself am praying through the medium of the wheel. The beauty of it all is that in my psychological inferiority I can think about whatever I want, I can yield to the most dirty and obscene fantasies, and it does not matter because - to use a good old Stalinist expression - whatever I am thinking, objectively I am praying. (31–32)

In this description of social practices removed from conscious thought, we see why cognitive behavioral therapy has become so popular today: people want to fix their mental problems without changing their underlying subjectivity; in other words, they want to be reprogrammed by the therapist so that they do not have to undergo the long process of psychoanalysis.[86] The idea here is to change the drives without changing the unconscious or the underlying demands for love, knowledge, and recognition.

What I have been arguing here is that Zizek ends up turning psychoanalysis into a cynical ideology that matches the cynical alienation of contemporary society: "This is how we should grasp the fundamental Lacanian proposition that psychoanalysis is not a psychology: the most intimate beliefs, even the most intimate emotions such as compassion, crying, sorrow, laughter, can be transferred, delegated to others without losing their sincerity" (32). In contemporary cynical conformity, one no longer has to believe in one's own beliefs since one creates a separation between behavior and subjectivity. Through this emptying of subjective content, thoughts and feelings are displaced onto the other; thus, the other feels and thinks in my place.[87] This voiding of the unconscious points to the pleasure principle and the desire to escape any feelings of tension or anxiety; when the other enjoys and thinks in my place, I can fulfil the death drive's push to use as little mental or physical energy as possible.[88] From this perspective, the reason why we are outsourcing our minds to computer technologies and our labor to automation is that we are finally able to realize the pleasure principle's law of inertia.[89]

Not only do we desire not to think or work, but we also seek to rid ourselves of the burden of feeling and enjoying: "The only correct answer would be that the other - embodied in the television set - is relieving us even of our duty to laugh - is laughing instead of us. So even if, tired from a hard day's stupid work, all evening we did nothing but gaze drowsily into the television screen, we can say afterwards that objectively, through the medium of the other, we had a really good time" (33). In referring to the laugh track in television comedies, Zizek affirms that we are driven to hand over responsibility for feeling, thinking, and enjoying to the other.[90] As a form of meaningless enjoyment, popular media gives us the opportunity to displace our internal lives onto an externalized representation. Of course, without internal thoughts and feelings, there can be no psychoanalysis, and here we see how Zizek's turn to Lacan results in making psychoanalysis itself impossible.

From Transference to Social Reality

One of the key ways that Zizek undermines psychoanalysis from within psychoanalysis is through his understanding of social belief:

> What we call 'social reality' is in the last resort an ethical construction; it is supported by a certain as if (we act as if we believe in the almightiness of bureaucracy, as if the President incarnates the will of the People, as if the Party expresses the objective interest of the working class ...). As soon as the belief (which, let us remind ourselves again, is definitely not to be conceived at a 'psychological' level: it is embodied, materialized, in the effective functioning of the social field) is lost, the very texture of the social field disintegrates. This was already articulated by Pascal, one of Althusser's principal points of reference, in his attempt to develop the concept of 'Ideological State Apparatuses'. According to Pascal, the interiority of our reasoning is determined by the external, nonsensical 'machine'--automatism of the signifier, of the symbolic network in which the subjects are caught. (65)

Zizek argues here that belief should not be conceived on a psychological level because it is embodied in social practices; however, Freud's concept of transference is a psychological explanation of how individuals accept cultural ideals and norms.[91] What allows us to trust others and believe what they say is that we transfer responsibility in order to escape our own freedom, guilt, and shame.

Moreover, the automatism of the signifier occurs on the level of the primary processes for Freud and not through social formations or drive-based behaviors. And yet, Zizek continues to conflate the primary processes, the unconscious, and social ideology:

> For we must make no mistake about ourselves: we are as much automaton as mind ... proofs only convince the mind; habit provides the strongest proofs and those that are most believed. It inclines the automaton, which leads the mind unconsciously along with it. Here Pascal produces the very Lacanian definition of the unconscious: 'the automaton (i.e. the dead, senseless letter), which leads the mind unconsciously [sans Ie savoir with it'. It follows, from this constitutively senseless character of the Law, that we must obey it not because it is just, good or even beneficial, but simply because it is the law--this tautology articulates the vicious circle of its authority, the fact that the last foundation of the Law's authority lies in its process of enunciation. (34–35)

While the automatic nature of the signifier in the mind relates to the way the primary processes structure our thoughts and perceptions, it is repression that determines the unconscious. Also, the social law is internalized through the super-ego and the ego-ideal through the process of transference and the threat of castration, and so it does not make sense to equate the automatic nature of the signifier with the law's authority.[92]

A possible reason for Zizek's desire to combine the unconscious, the primary process, and transference together is that he wants to posit that our submission to the social order is not based on subjectivity: "The only real obedience, then, is an 'external' one: obedience out of conviction is not real obedience because it is already 'mediated' through our subjectivity—that is, we are not really obeying the authority but simply following our judgement, which tells us that the authority deserves to be obeyed in so far as it is good, wise, beneficent" (35). Whereas Zizek opposes subjectivity and submission here, Lacan defines the subject as being excluded by language and society through its inclusion.[93] In fact, for psychoanalytic practice and theory, it is necessary to distinguish five types of subjection: (1) the loss of intentional control with the primary processes; (2) the loss of awareness in repression; (3) the submission of the self to the Other in transference; (4) the loss of self-control with the drives; and (5) the submission of the self to reality in the reality principle.[94] When we do not make these distinction, we lose the meaning of psychoanalysis itself.

Notes

1. Žižek, Slavoj. *The sublime object of ideology*. Verso Books, 2019.
2. Freud, Sigmund. *Civilization and its discontents*. Broadview Press, 2015.
3. Lacan, Jacques, and Jacques-Alain Miller. *The ethics of psychoanalysis 1959-1960: The seminar of Jacques Lacan*. Routledge, 2013.
4. Freud, Sigmund. *The future of an illusion*. Broadview Press, 2012.
5. Althusser, Louis. "Ideology and ideological state apparatuses (notes towards an investigation)." *The anthropology of the state: A reader* 9.1 (2006): 86–98.
6. Reinhard, Kenneth. "Lacan and Monotheism: Psychoanalysis and the Traversal of Cultural Fantasy." *Jouvert: A Journal of Postcolonial Studies* 3.1–2 (1999).
7. Shepherdson, Charles. *Lacan and the Limits of Language*. Fordham University Press, 2009.
8. Clemens, Justin, et al. *Jacques Lacan and the Other Side of Psychoanalysis: Reflections on Seminar XVII, Sic Vi*. Duke University Press, 2006.
9. Lacan, Jacques, Alan Sheridan, and Malcolm Bowie. "The function and field of speech and language in psychoanalysis." *Écrits*. Routledge, 2020. 33–125.
10. Rieff, Philip. *Freud: The mind of the moralist*. University of Chicago Press, 1979.
11. Davis, Robert Con. "Pedagogy, Lacan, and the Freudian subject." *College English* 49.7 (1987): 749–755.
12. Lacan, Jacques, Jacques-Alain Ed Miller, and Bruce Trans Fink. *Desire and its interpretation: The seminar of Jacques Lacan, Book VI*. Polity Press, 2019.

13. Samuels, Robert. "Žižek's Rhetorical Matrix: The Symptomatic Enjoyment of Postmodern Academic Writing." *JAC* (2002): 327–354.
14. Samuels, Robert. "Catharsis: The politics of enjoyment." *Zizek and the rhetorical unconscious*. Palgrave Macmillan, Cham, 2020. 7–31.
15. Voruz, Véronique, and Bogdan Wolf, eds. *The Later Lacan: An Introduction*. SUNY Press, 2012.
16. Miller, Jacques-Alain. "Interpretation in reverse." *Bulletin de NLS* 4 (2008): 69–75.
17. Lacan, Jacques. "The seminar of Jacques Lacan: Book XX: Encore: 1972-1973." (2011).
18. Lacan, Jacques, Alan Sheridan, and Malcolm Bowie. "The function and field of speech and language in psychoanalysis." *Écrits*. Routledge, 2020. 33–125.
19. Badiou, Alain, and Elisabeth Roudinesco. *Jacques Lacan, past and present*. Columbia University Press, 2014.
20. Byram, T. "Visions of the Self Conflict and Deficit: Toward an Integrative Vision of the Self." *American Journal of Psychoanalysis* 55.3 (1995): 275.
21. Freud, Sigmund. "Beyond the pleasure principle." *The Standard Edition of the Complete Psychological Works of Sigmund Freud, Volume XVIII (1920-1922): Beyond the Pleasure Principle, Group Psychology and Other Works*. 1955. 1–64.
22. Evans, Dylan. "From Kantian ethics to mystical experience: An exploration of jouissance." *Key concepts of Lacanian psychoanalysis*. Routledge, 2018. 1–28.
23. Braunstein, Néstor. "Desire and Jouissance in the Teachings of Lacan." *The Cambridge Companion to Lacan* (2003): 102–115.
24. Black, David M. "Mapping a Detour: Why did Freud Speak of a Death Drive? 1." *British Journal of Psychotherapy* 18.2 (2001): 185–198.
25. Samuels, Robert. "The pleasure principle and the death drive." *Freud for the twenty-first century*. Palgrave Pivot, Cham, 2019. 17–25.
26. Aycock, Alan. "Derrida/Fort-da: deconstructing play." *Postmodern Culture* 3.2 (1993).
27. Samuels, Robert. "Logos, global justice, and the reality principle." *Zizek and the rhetorical unconscious*. Palgrave Macmillan, Cham, 2020. 65–86.
28. Freud, Sigmund. *Civilization and its discontents*. Broadview Press, 2015.
29. Freud, Sigmund. "The ego and the id (1923)." *TACD Journal* 17.1 (1989): 5–22.

30. Marcuse, Herbert. *Eros and civilization: A philosophical inquiry into Freud.* Routledge, 2012.
31. Freud, Sigmund. "Project for a scientific psychology (1950 [1895])." *The Standard Edition of the Complete Psychological Works of Sigmund Freud, Volume I (1886-1899): Pre-Psycho-Analytic Publications and Unpublished Drafts.* 1966. 281–391.
32. Benvenuto, Bice. *Once upon a Time: The Infant in Lacanian Theory 1.* Routledge, 2018.
33. Žižek, Slavoj. *For they know not what they do: Enjoyment as a political factor.* Verso, 2002.
34. Samuels, Robert. "Catharsis: The politics of enjoyment." *Zizek and the rhetorical unconscious.* Palgrave Macmillan, Cham, 2020. 7–31.
35. Samuels, Robert. "Logos, global justice, and the reality principle." *Zizek and the rhetorical unconscious.* Palgrave Macmillan, Cham, 2020. 65–86.
36. Sherratt, Yvonne. "Adorno's concept of the self: A marriage of Freud and Hegelian Marxism." *Revue internationale de philosophie* 1 (2004): 101–117.
37. Sharpe, Matthew. "What's left in Žižek? The antinomies of Žižek's socio-political reason." *Traversing the Fantasy.* Routledge, 2017. 147–168.
38. Hell, Julia. "Remnants of totalitarianism: Hannah Arendt, Heiner Müller, Slavoj Žižek, and the re-invention of politics." *telos* 2006.136 (2006): 76–103.
39. Ferguson, Jonathan. "Translation Review Essay:"Autour de Slavoj Žižek: Psychanalyse, Marxisme, Idealisme Allemand."(Benoît Guillette, Université du Québec à Montréal)." *International Journal of Žižek Studies* 4.4 (2016).
40. Scheff, Thomas J. "Shame in self and society." *Symbolic interaction* 26.2 (2003): 239–262.
41. Mróz, Piotr, and Łukasz Śliwa. "On diverse understandings of the notion of tolerance: behaviorism versus psychoanalysis.' (2016).
42. Freud, Sigmund, James Strachey, and Anna Freud. *The psychopathology of everyday life:(1901).* Hogarth Press: Institute of Psycho-Analysis, 1978.
43. Rensmann, Lars. *The politics of unreason: The Frankfurt School and the origins of modern antisemitism.* Suny Press, 2017.
44. Zetzel, Elizabeth, R. "1965: Additional notes upon a case of obsessional neurosis: Freud 1909." *International Journal of Psycho-Analysis* 47 (1966): 123–129.

45. Freud, Sigmund. "Hysterical phantasies and their relation to bisexuality." *The Standard Edition of the Complete Psychological Works of Sigmund Freud, Volume IX (1906-1908): Jensen's 'Gradiva'and Other Works*. 1959. 155–166.
46. Flemming, Gregory C. "In the Beginning… Was the Act!: Zizek, Marx, and the Question of Form." (2014).
47. Marx, Karl, and Friedrich Engels. *The communist manifesto*. Phoemixx Classics Ebooks, 2021.
48. Samuels, Robert. "Žižek's Rhetorical Matrix: The Symptomatic Enjoyment of Postmodern Academic Writing." *JAC* (2002): 327–354.
49. Baudrillard, Jean. *The transparency of evil: Essays on extreme phenomena*. Verso, 1993.
50. Tomšič, Samo. *The capitalist unconscious: Marx and Lacan*. Verso Books, 2015.
51. Freud, Sigmund. "A special type of choice of object made by men (Contributions to the psychology of love I)." *The Standard Edition of the Complete Psychological Works of Sigmund Freud, Volume XI (1910): Five Lectures on Psycho-Analysis, Leonardo da Vinci and Other Works*. 1957. 163–176.
52. Freud, Sigmund. *Fetishism*. Routledge, 2017.
53. Dant, Tim. "Fetishism and the social value of objects 1." *The Sociological Review* 44.3 (1996): 495–516.
54. Lacan, Jacques, and Jacques-Alain Miller. *The ethics of psychoanalysis 1959-1960: The seminar of Jacques Lacan*. Routledge, 2013.
55. Freud, Sigmund. "Group psychology and the analysis of the ego." *The Standard Edition of the Complete Psychological Works of Sigmund Freud, Volume XVIII (1920-1922): Beyond the Pleasure Principle, Group Psychology and Other Works*. 1955. 65–144.
56. Sweezy, Paul M., and Maurice Dobb. "The transition from feudalism to capitalism." *Science & Society* (1950): 134–167.
57. Holton, Robert J. "Marxist theories of social change and the transition from feudalism to capitalism." *Theory and society* 10.6 (1981): 833–867.
58. Freud, Sigmund. *On the universal tendency to debasement in the sphere of love*. Read Books Ltd, 2014.
59. Samuels, Robert. *New media, cultural studies, and critical theory after postmodernism: Automodernity from Zizek to Laclau*. Springer, 2009.
60. Baudrillard, Jean. *Impossible exchange*. Verso Trade, 2012.
61. Nasio, Juan-David. *Book of Love and Pain, The: Thinking at the Limit with Freud and Lacan*. Suny Press, 2012.

62. Freud, Sigmund, and James Strachey. *The interpretation of dreams*. New York: Gramercy Books, 1996.
63. Dundes, Alan. "Binary opposition in myth: The Propp/Levi-Strauss debate in retrospect." *Western folklore* (1997): 39–50.
64. Freud, Sigmund. *Totem And Taboo: Some Points of Agreement between the Mental Lives of Savages and*. Routledge, 2013.
65. Freud, Sigmund. "The dissolution of the Oedipus complex." *The Standard Edition of the Complete Psychological Works of Sigmund Freud, Volume XIX (1923-1925): The Ego and the Id and Other Works*. 1961. 171–180.
66. Freud, Sigmund. "Some psychical consequences of the anatomical distinction between the sexes." *Strachey, trans. and ed* 19.253 (1925): 19.
67. Lacan, Jacques, Alan Sheridan, and Malcolm Bowie. "The Subversion of the Subject and the Dialectic of Desire in the Freudian Unconscious." *Écrits*. Routledge, 2020. 323–360.
68. Skinner, Burrhus Frederic. *The selection of behavior: The operant behaviorism of BF Skinner: Comments and consequences*. CUP Archive, 1988.
69. Hoedemaekers, Casper. "The fantasy of control: Behaviourist transgressions of neoliberal subjectivity." *Psychoanalysis, Culture & Society* 24.3 (2019): 303–322.
70. Žižek, Slavoj. *For they know not what they do: Enjoyment as a political factor*. Verso, 2002.
71. Samuels, Robert. "Žižek's Rhetorical Matrix: The Symptomatic Enjoyment of Postmodern Academic Writing." *JAC* (2002): 327–354.
72. Boucher, Geoff. "The Antinomies of Slavoj Zizek." *telos*2004.129 (2004): 151–172.
73. Samuels, Robert. "Lacan after Žižek: Self-Reflexivity in the Automodern Enjoyment of Psychoanalysis." *International Journal of Žižek Studies* 2.4 (2016).
74. Johnston, Adrian. *A New German Idealism: Hegel, Žižek, and Dialectical Materialism*. Columbia University Press, 2018.
75. Brüne, Martin. "Borderline Personality Disorder Why 'fast and furious'?." *Evolution, medicine, and public health* 2016.1 (2016): 52–66.
76. Láng, András. "Borderline personality organization predicts Machiavellian interpersonal tactics." *Personality and Individual Differences* 80 (2015): 28–31.
77. Pines, Malcolm. "Borderline Personality Organisation." *Psychotherapy and psychosomatics* 25.1/6 (1975): 58–62.

78. Stone, Michael H. "Incest, Freud's seduction theory, and borderline personality." *Journal of the American Academy of Psychoanalysis* 20.2 (1992): 167–181.
79. Sloterdijk, Peter, Michael Eldred, and Leslie A. Adelson. "Cynicism: the twilight of false consciousness." *New German Critique* 33 (1984): 190–206.
80. Robinson, Andrew, and Simon Tormey. "Zizek's Marx:'Sublime Object'or a'Plague of Fantasies'?." *Historical Materialism* 14.3 (2007): 145.
81. Samuels, Robert. "Žižek's Rhetorical Matrix: The Symptomatic Enjoyment of Postmodern Academic Writing." *JAC* (2002): 327–354.
82. Rizvi, Shireen L., and Marsha M. Linehan. "The treatment of maladaptive shame in borderline personality disorder: A pilot study of "opposite action"." *Cognitive and Behavioral Practice* 12.4 (2005): 437–447.
83. Reed, James. "Mechanical man: John Broadus Watson and the beginnings of behaviorism." *Science* 244.4910 (1989): 1386–1388.
84. Hurry, Anne, Jack Novick, and Kerry Kelly Novick. "freud's concept of projection." *Journal of Child Psychotherapy* 4.2 (1976): 75–88.
85. Weber, Max, and Damion Searls. *Charisma and disenchantment: The vocation lectures*. NYRB Classics, 2020.
86. Snell, Robert. "L'Anti-Livre noir de la psychoanalyse. CBT in French/Lacanian perspective." (2008).
87. Pfaller, Robert. *Interpassivity: The aesthetics of delegated enjoyment*. Edinburgh University Press, 2017.
88. Samuels, Robert. "The pleasure principle and the death drive." *Freud for the twenty-first century*. Palgrave Pivot, Cham, 2019. 17–25.
89. Noble, David F. "Digital diploma mills: The automation of higher education." *Science as culture* 7.3 (1998): 355–368.
90. Pfaller, Robert. "Interpassivity and misdemeanors. The analysis of ideology and the Zizekian toolbox." *Revue internationale de philosophie* 3 (2012): 421–438.
91. Samuels, Robert. "Ethos, Transference, and Liberal Cynicism." *Zizek and the Rhetorical Unconscious*. Palgrave Macmillan, Cham, 2020. 49–63.
92. Samuels, Robert. "The unconscious and the primary processes." *Freud for the twenty-first century*. Palgrave Pivot, Cham, 2019. 27–42.
93. Lacan, Jacques, Jacques-Alain Miller, and Alan Sheridan. *The four fundamental concepts of psycho-analysis*. Routledge, 2018.
94. Bracher, Mark, et al., eds. *Lacanian theory of discourse: Subject, structure, and society*. NYU Press, 1994.

7

Misunderstanding Psychoanalysis from the Left

This chapter examines how certain tendencies of contemporary Left-wing politics and subjectivity can undermine our understanding of psychoanalysis within psychoanalysis discourse. In critiquing the book *Intersectionality and Relational Psychoanalysis*, I hope to show the ways the repression of analytic neutrality results in the reinforcement of a dualistic model of subjectivity and analysis.[1] I will also address the relation between the psychoanalysis of culture and psychoanalytic treatment. One of my main arguments is that the theory and the practice of psychoanalysis represents an encounter between a universal model and the singularity of individual experience and thought, and the best way to respect this dialectic is to return to Freud's fundamental concepts.[2]

Warning: Reader Be Aware

Before I look into this topic, it is important to point out how the psychopathology of some contemporary Left-wing ideology makes it difficult to approach this subject.[3] Since so much of the discourse of the Left relies on articulating a clear distinction between the good, innocent victim and

R. Samuels, *(Mis)Understanding Freud with Lacan, Zizek, and Neuroscience*, The Palgrave Lacan Series, https://doi.org/10.1007/978-3-031-13327-5_7

the evil Other, any criticism of this discourses can be seen as an effort to blame the victims of persecution.[4] Moreover, the highly emotional way that the antagonism between the self and the other is represented and lived, makes it hard to examine this discourse in a scientific or neutral manner. In fact, as we shall see, a hallmark of this ideology and subjectivity is the rejection of neutrality itself.[5]

One of Freud's most important and controversial ideas was his theory that people often imagine scenes of victimization.[6] However, many people inside and outside of psychoanalysis have rejected this theory because it appears to dismiss the suffering of people who have been truly victimized as it lets the victimizer off the hook.[7] Yet, from a psychoanalytic perspective, we can never know for sure what happened in someone's life, but what we do need to consider is how one responds to real and imagined suffering.[8] The questions of identity and identification are then key to the theory of psychoanalysis, but in the actual practice, identity and identification have to be called into question through the privileging of analytic neutrality, free association, and unconscious material.[9]

It is my thesis that these basic aspects of analytic practice are rejected and repressed through a return to a pre-Freudian understanding of therapy.[10] On the most basic level, the therapists and analysts in *Intersectionality and Relational Psychoanalysis* see their roles as centered on providing knowledge, love, and recognition to their patients. In other words, instead of working through the transference, they aim to strengthen it by responding to their patients' fundamental demands. Not only does this mode of treatment reinforce defensive forms of identity and identification, but it reduces the analytic relationship to a dualistic structure where the analyst can be either a source for identification or a cause for frustration.[11]

As Lacan insists, the dualistic view of the analytic relationship blocks the emergence of unconscious material as it substantiates primitive fantasies on an imaginary level.[12] Since the goal is to expose and move beyond these limiting mental representations, the analyst has to remain neutral so that the patient can speak without censorship or thinking about what the analyst is thinking.[13] Of course, this is a very strange type of relationship, and it is perhaps this strangeness that prevents therapists and analysts from accepting the foundations of psychoanalysis itself.

Another related issue that we find throughout this book is the conflict between the academic application of psychoanalysis to culture and the use of theory to shape treatment. Although I do believe that psychoanalysis has many important things to say about race, class, gender, and other social issues, there is an important difference between examining culture and psychoanalytic treatment.[14] Since the analyst has to remain neutral in order to enable free association, the analyst cannot be a social critic when he or she is engaged in the analytic process. It is therefore necessary to recognize a clear distinction between using analytic concepts to define the role of the analyst and the employment of these same concepts to examine social and cultural issues.[15] In fact, as we shall see, many problems arise when we do not make this distinction, and we begin to see the analyst as playing the role of the political activist.[16] However, if the analyst has to suspend judgment and not feed the patient's demand for love, recognition, and knowledge, then the analyst has to also suspend political analysis and intervention within the clinical relationship.[17]

Identity in Analysis

In their introduction to their book, Max Belkin and Cleonie White point out that "the contributing authors explore how similarities and differences among the patient's and analyst's gender, race, and sexual orientation can be acknowledged, challenged, and negotiated" (iii). In highlighting the role played by these social categories in the relationship between the therapist and the patient, the authors take a decisive step away from both analytic neutrality and free association since they believe that the analyst must be constantly aware of his or her own identity.[18] Moreover, instead of seeing analysis as centered on discovering unknown unconscious material, there is a tendency to examine fixed identities and identifications.

One of the main ways that the focus on fixated markers of sexual, racial, and class identities is evident in this collection of essays is through the notion that patients want to be analyzed by people who belong to the same identity group.[19] We see this identity-based understanding of the transference in the following passage:

> One day, a couple of months into my work with a Mexican-American graduate student named Ana, I casually inquired about her reactions to me. First, she offered her usual "I am glad that you share my background in philosophy and can understand me." But then I heard something new and baffling: "I had to stop watching House of Cards recently," added Ana with an anxious laugh. "Kevin Spacey looks too much like you. I mean, like you, he acts straight, even though he is totally gay." Taken aback, I asked Ana, "Are you wondering whether I am gay or straight?" To my surprise, instead of saying something reassuring and deferential, which used to be her habit, Ana continued: "When I googled you before our first session, I found out that you are from Russia, that you are Jewish and gay. But now I read you as a white, privileged straight man. I don't hear your accent. (7)

As we see from this example, the neutrality of the analyst is challenged by the desire of the patient to place the analyst in a particular set of social and cultural identity markers.[20] Since the patient wants to find an ego ideal that can validate their own ideal ego, they seek to place the analyst and themselves in defined social categories.[21] In this structure, the narcissistic transference is solidified as the fundamental demand for recognition is satisfied. While this type of relationship may appear to be soothing to both the analyst and the patient, the question is if it is effective in allowing for the emergence of unknown unconscious material?[22]

As Freud discovered, the more that an analyst reveals about himself or herself, the more the patient will either identify with the analyst or reject the analyst.[23] In creating this dualistic relation centered on the binary choice of acceptance or rejection, a situation of control and pleasure is produced, but the cost of this narcissistic relation is a limiting of what can be said or thought.[24] Unfortunately, many therapists and analysts do not accept the need for neutrality, and so they fall into the habit of reinscribing the strangeness of the analytic relationship back into the common way of communicating and interacting. For example, Belkin mentions how he answers his patients' questions in a direct manner that enables them to know what he thinks and likes: "upon entering the waiting room to greet Ana, I found her immersed in reading White Girls (2013) by Hilton Als. Ana inquired whether I had already read it, and after learning that I had not, told me to check it out" (7). Although it may appear that no harm is done to the analytic process by simply answering a question about a book, Lacan argued that each particular demand is actually supported by a fundamental desire for love, recognition, and understanding, which forms the basis of the transference.[25] By responding to any direct question with a direct answer, the therapist is then reinforcing the transference, and not only is the fundamental demand not allowed to emerge, but the analytic relationship is reabsorbed into an imaginary, dualistic structure.[26]

Since this collection is centered on a relational approach to psychoanalysis, it is not surprising that the analysts and therapists continue to see the analytic experience as a dualistic encounter, but it is important for us to examine how this conception of analysis misunderstands Freud's key concepts and their role in guiding the actions of the analyst. Due to the fact that Freud learned that people would only be able to discover new repressed material if they stopped thinking about what the analyst thought about them, it is essential for the analyst to not only have an open mind but also to resist disclosing their thoughts, feelings, and personal information.[27] However, therapists and analysts like Belkin believe that self-disclosure enables a more meaningful and supportive relationship: "In retrospect, I view Ana's question about my gayness as an invitation to be queer together: to transcend the rigid binary categories of homosexual and heterosexual, white versus person of color, male or female, to create new meanings and possibilities for each other" (Both patient and analyst can only access their dissociated parts via participating in jointly created enactments and by examining their personal contributions to them)" (9). This notion of the analyst and patient co-creating meaning together over their shared identities is in direct conflict with the Freudian idea that the neutrality of the analyst allows the patient to discover things on his or her own.[28] Moreover, like the concept of countertransference, the idea of enactment is often used to signal that the subjectivity of the analyst is as important as the subjectivity of the patient.[29] Thus, instead of the analyst working hard to suspend judgment and present a blank screen for projection and displacement, many contemporary therapists and analysts stress the need for the analysts to constantly judge their own internal thoughts and feelings.[30]

This notion that the therapist and the patient have to both disclose what they are thinking at all times perverts the fundamental analytic process and feeds a sense of narcissism for both the patent and the analyst.[31] Since both want to be seen as the one who knows, the only way to avoid conflict is through the process of imaginary identification. Belkin reveals this issue in the following way: "Articulating and exploring the differences and similarities between me and Ana seemed not only important, but also fraught. According to Russell Meares (1993), "the therapist's state of mind should resemble that to which the patient's should be moving" (p. 184)" (10). In this melding of two minds, the goal appears to be for the patient to identify with the ideal movement of the analyst's own mind.[32] It is hard to see how this process enables discovery or individual autonomy.

In light of Belkin's promotion of an imaginary mode of transference and identification, it is strange that he still wants to insist that the goal of analysis is to foster curiosity and personal freedom: "While curious uncertainty never completely supplants defensive not knowing, the goal of psychotherapy is to foster curiosity and expand our relational freedom at the expense of narrative and interpersonal rigidity (Stern, 2015)" (15). Since the way to promote independence and open inquiry is through the suspension of identity and identification, the question remains why Belkin is still focused on the very rigid categories he now sees as stifling the analytic process.[33] In fact, he offers an interesting metaphor for the analytic process itself: "Thus, psychoanalytic inquiry is akin to driving a car: one is always wondering where one is headed, while at the same time remembering that one always has blind spots" (15). This notion of wondering where you are going and recognizing that one has blind spots is an apt description for what it often feels like to be an analyst and a patient. The problem is that rigid markers of identity and identification often block free association, and so in many ways, psychoanalysis is in conflict with the application of identity politics in the clinic.[34]

If we want to be open to seeing all people without judgment, then it makes no sense to focus on race, class, and gender markers. Of course, this colorblind approach to social categories of discrimination can be attacked for denying systemic oppression and the suffering of the victims of prejudice, but my argument here is that for benefit of analytic treatment, all social and political effects can be voiced and felt through the speech of the patient; however, the analyst should avoid substantiating any form of identity and identification.[35] From this perspective, the analytic relation is not symmetrical, and yet Belkin wants to insist on an imaginary dualism: "From the one-person perspective, the patient is in the driving seat, while the analyst is a passenger-observer (Wachtel, 2008). However, in the two-person psychology that informs my thinking about the intersections among ethnicity, gender, and sexual identity, the "analysis-mobile" comes with two brake pedals and two steering wheels; both individuals are simultaneously a passenger and a driver; each of them is an observing participant (Fiscalini, 2004)" (15). The problem with this symmetrical formulation is that is does not accept the fundamental lack of participation of the analyst, while it reinforces the narcissistic relation of identification and rivalry: "Through a joint exploration of their emotional exchanges in the "here and now," patient and analyst can describe both the privileged and marginalized aspects of their identities" (16). As I have been arguing, the goal of analytic treatment is to use free association in order to uncover the patient's repressed unconscious material. When the analyst openly discusses his or her thoughts and emotions, neutrality is lost, and the patient seeks to transfer responsibility for knowledge onto the analyst who is idealized as the one who is supposed to know.[36] In fact, Belkin does realize one of the pitfalls of this bonding over knowledge, identity, and meaning: "From the onset of treatment, as we now suspect, the two of us had been ensconced in a comfortable illusion that we understood both ourselves and the other person" (17). On a fundamental level, psychoanalysis tells us that we never fully understand ourselves or other people, and so our sense of understanding and knowledge always has an imaginary aspect where we fill in the gaps and cover over the lacks.[37]

The analyst's neutrality, then, is in part derived from an acceptance of the conflict between two consciousness and the need to protect against the projection of meaning and understanding onto the other in the transference.[38] The analyst has to also refrain from satisfying the drives and demands of the patient as the psychoanalyst resists seeking narcissistic gratification from the patient, and yet Belkin shows how hard it can be to maintain this type of relationship: "Upon arriving to our first meeting,

Ana glanced at the office décor and my clothes and remarked that aesthetics mean a lot to both of us. I was flattered that this attractive, sophisticated young woman chose me as her therapist" (18). It is important to stress that the analyst seeks to remove himself or herself from this relation of admiration and aesthetics by sitting behind the patient.[39] In staying out of view, the analyst becomes more of a blank screen, which enables the suspending of the imaginary mirroring narcissistic structure. In contrast to Kohut, Lacan emphasizes the need to not feed the patient's demand for idealization or mirroring, and so he claims that the analyst becomes an object lacking a specular image.[40]

Belkin is aware of the problems contained in a narcissistic transference, but he appears to be unable to fully commit to the position of the analyst: "During the first phase of treatment, Ana was open to my questions and frequently responded to my observations and interpretations with a reassuring "Yeah, it's definitely true." Although my narcissistic side was basking in what felt like Ana's approval, something felt a bit off" (18). As Belkin indicates, the analyst may desire to be admired for his knowledge, but even if the patent appears to demand this type of relationship, there is usually a part of the subject that resists this idealization of the other. In fact, Lacan stresses that in the imaginary structure of narcissism, we often resent the person we idealize.[41] Moreover, when the patient transfers responsibility for knowing and care onto the analyst, the patient often feels ambivalent about handing power over to another person.[42]

In fact, when working with narcissistic obsessional patients, it is very apparent that behind the patient's desire to comply with the analyst, we find an underlying resistance.[43] Since narcissists want their ideal ego to be recognized by an idealized Other, they become anxious and upset when this Other fails to fulfill this position:

> "Ana," I offered, trying to sound casual, "I am a bit surprised that you seem always in agreement with everything that I say. I can't always be right." Ana smiled and admitted that she wanted to please me. Moreover, just as she does in other social settings, she had compiled a mental list of what makes me tick, and strategically complimented my plants and my outfits. And then Ana secretly disdained me (just like she despised others) for being so vain and gullible. "Why do I need to destroy people?" she later asked both of us. "I feel bad about being manipulative." (18)

This conflict between wanting to comply with others and the resentment of others shows the fundamental ambivalence structuring narcissistic relationships; on the one hand, the subject wants to be recognized as being good by conforming to social expectations, but on the other hand, this conformity requires a sacrifice of the self, which is resented.[44] Furthermore, when a demand is made to the Other for love, recognition, and understanding, what is really desired is for the Other to submit to the will of the subject.[45]

The only way to break out of this narcissistic relationship is for the analyst to refuse to play the part of the one who responds to the demands of the patient.[46] Of course, it can be quite difficult to constantly resist satisfying the patient, but the only way to allow for a new type of relationship to emerge is to expose the underlying demands of the subject.[47] On a basic level, the analysis must always remain strange and uncomfortable because this position suspends the usual ways of communicating and interacting. The conflict, then, that we find between identity politics and psychoanalysis is that the analyst has to bracket his or her identity in order to enable the patient the ability to explore the relation between social categories and subjectivity in an open and free way.[48] However, as we see from the next passage, Belkin does not trust this process, and so he returns to an imaginary rivalry between two opposed victim identities: "I am a marginalized Latina, an underdog with a queer sensibility; you are a privileged, straight-acting white man," thought Ana. "No. I am the underdog here. After all, I am a gay Jewish immigrant, while you are a straight American woman from a rich family," protested my inner voice" (19). In this conflict between social identities, the possibility for analytic neutrality is lost, and as Belkin adds, the result is a competition for moral goodness: "In retrospect, it seems that both Ana and I were secretly jostling for some sort of moral superiority" (19). Here, we see the dangers of maintaining the analytic relationship on the level of narcissistic identification and idealization: The analyst cannot help but to feed the underlying negative transference as a constant-sum relationship is established where one person wins and the other loses.[49] The only solution is for the analyst to simply refuse to play this imaginary game.

Belkin's text does provide a deep insight into the reasons why most forms of therapy and analysis that move away from neutrality fail, and these reasons have a lot to do with inherent tensions within identity politics. Although this form of political activism does play a vital role in expanding democratic rights and protections, it often can become counter-productive when it becomes fixated on a binary battle between idealized innocent victims and demonized perpetrators.[50] Instead of affirming the fundamental ambivalence of the subject, a splitting occurs where one is either idealized or debased. Furthermore, as Freud found in his exploration of masochistic fantasies and psycho-somatic disorders, the person who is suffering often feels that their aggression towards others is justified as they feel morally superior due to their victim status.[51] Since in this fantasy structure, the victim is always good and innocent, and you cannot criticize the victim, revenge is justified, while reality testing and moral reasoning can be suspended.[52]

As is evident in Belkin's discussion of his work with Ana, a focus on intersectionality in the clinic can result in the formation of defensive identities and a splitting off of undesired parts of the self and other: "Both Ana and I seemed married to our narrow and rigid perceptions of our own selves and of each other. Neither of us wanted to concede that we might be in any way the more privileged person. Moreover, focusing on the presumed privileged parts of the other allowed each of us to feel self-righteous" (19). In this dualistic structure, there is always the calculation of a moral imbalance that in turn justifies a reductive understanding of the self and the other. For Belkin, the solution to this imaginary rivalry is the embracing of a shared process: "Until she and I became curious collaborators united by a common project, we kept swapping the roles of the domineering and the subjugated (Benjamin, 2004)" (19). Once again, the problem with this formulation is that the analytic relationship is neither symmetrical nor common.[53]

As Ana herself discovers, even when people ask for help, they often resent the helper because it gives the other relational power: "At the same time, she was reluctant to acknowledge that working with me was helpful to her. "Telling you about my sadness feels like giving into your expectations. You'll have a one up on me," she mused" (20). The desire for autonomy and freedom thus runs into the demand for love, recognition, and understanding, and so it is important for the analyst to avoid reinforcing these roles in the transference even though they often represent a key to the treatment. Since the very act of the patient coming to seek help represents a fundamental transference demand, they analyst should not have to feed this imaginary relationship; rather the analyst desires the patient to free associate, and this requires analytic neutrality and the non-involvement in the inevitable transference.[54] Furthermore, since one of the goals of analysis is to work through the transference, it is necessary to make sure that it comes from the patient and not the analyst. In other words, by being a blank screen, the analyst makes it clear that the relationship is produced through the patient's imaginary fantasies and unconscious demands.[55]

Although it does appear that Belkin was able to make much progress in uncovering Ana's underlying subjectivity, his participation in her imaginary understanding blocked a full working through of the transference. As he admits himself, his self-disclosures served to provide a source of identification for his patient: "I might have inadvertently modeled for Ana that it was relatively safe to come emotionally undone in our relationship, to appear unsophisticated, unsure, anxious, and even ashamed. I shared with Ana the contents of my mind, including my efforts to tolerate shame" (25). The problem with this process of modeling thought and behavior for the patient is that it feeds both the narcissistic idealization of the analyst and the defensive resistance to analysis itself.[56] Belkin expresses the ambivalence generated by this approach in the following manner: "In return, Ana explored her ambivalent reaction to my self-disclosure. While she appreciated my honesty, she was also feeling vindicated, victorious, superior – and she felt guilty about it" (26). Due to the nature of neurotic ambivalence, even if the analyst thinks that he or she is doing something good and helpful for the patient, the subject may resent it, and any self-disclosure by the analyst will be used by the patient in the private court of moral judgment.[57]

From Lacan's perspective, the analyst must take on the role of being the object for the patient, and Belkin does seem to concur with this notion: "Before Ana and I began to play together in a metaphorical space between fantasy and reality (Winnicott, 1971), Ana tended to use me like a transitional object, a teddy bear: something to cuddle, hate, and mutilate, but not destroy. While I did not particularly enjoy being treated that way, I felt safe enough to continue, and I let Ana know that" (26).

Although Belkin does afform being a transitional object for Ana, he betrays this position by letting his patient know that he knows what is going on. Since an object cannot know or communicate, it becomes the presence of an unknowable thing within analysis, and this reminder of the real serves the purpose of showing the arbitrary nature of the object of our desires.[58] Due to the perverse nature of human sexuality, any object or activity can be sexualized, and thus the objects we desire have no inherent value.[59] In a parallel way, the transference reveals how the relationship between the patient and the analyst is derived through the primary processes of the patient, and so the position of neutrality clears the ground for a full exploration of repressed unconscious material.

How Identity Politics Affects Clinical Practice

In examining Belkin's work, I have stressed the many ways that the analyst's focus on identity politics can affect the ability to maintain analytic neutrality. By looking at several other authors from the same collection, we find a similar conflict between Freud's model of analysis and the desire to apply issues concerning, race, gender, class, and sexual orientation within an object relations conception of therapy.[60] For instance, in Avgi Saketopoulou's "Minding the Gap," we are told that "in clinical work with transgender (and otherwise queer) patients, considerations of race and class are not only important facets of the work: they are the work" (33). By claiming that the form and content of therapy is defined by these identity markers and issues, the possibility for exploration by the patient appears to be limited since free association requires speaking about anything and everything.[61] Once again, the point is not that these identity issues are not important; the problem emerges when they are the only things that matters in analysis.

As the theories and practice of identity politics continue to spread throughout culture and academic discourse, what we often find is that these vital issues begin to dominate every other possible area of consideration.[62] For example, in her chapter "Subordinated Selves," Hannah Pocock questions the goal of fostering individual autonomy in analysis because individualism has been coded as masculine within Western culture: “Benjamin (1988) has noted that the Western assumption of the primacy of individualism in human development is implicitly gendered. Rationality and autonomy (qualities attributed to the father in traditional psychoanalytic frameworks) are celebrated, while empathy, emotion, and other human capacities deemed feminine are devalued” (66). Since reason and autonomy have often been attached to masculine identity, Pocock seeks to affirm the opposite traits as essential to a feminist mode of psychoanalysis. In this postmodern reversal of premodern hierarchies and binaries, the same categories of essentialized identity are being used, but now the debased attributes are idealized, while the former ideals are critiqued.[63] The problem with this strategy is that it remains tied to the same rigid identity categories as it reinforces a reductive binary logic.

What the postmodern reversal of premodern values refuses to recognize is the importance of the modern effort to suspend these categories through the affirmation of universality, neutrality, objectivity, and reason.[64] At the foundation of modern democratic law is the necessary but impossible ideal of equal treatment regardless of race, class, gender, or sexual orientation.[65] Of course, the law often fails to live up to these ideals, but we judge its failures in relation to this ideal. While it is true that many postmodern social movements to promote minority rights seek to expand and correct universal human rights, the central problem occurs when these movements become so fixated on protecting their particular identities that they reject the very notions of universality, equality, and neutrality.[66] As we saw in the passage above, this rejection of modern principles often includes a rejection of reason and individual autonomy since they are seen as being the products of white European males.

Freud’s conceptions of science, the reality principle, free association, and analytic neutrality are all being called into question because from the perspective of postmodern identity politics, these principles are all coded as masculine, white, and straight.[67] Here we witness the ways that political ideologies and movements can affect how people practice psychoanalysis since the rejection of its core concepts and practices is motivated by a particular political discourse. Instead of seeing neutrality as a bias against bias, it is interpreted as a masculine value promoted to erase issues concerning race, class, gender, and sexual orientation.[68] As Pocock insists, analytic neutrality has to be rejected because it is just a cover for masculine power: "While these systems cloak themselves in the mantle of neutrality, Benjamin argues that it is precisely the disproportionate valuing of rationality and objective indifference to personal need that are the trademarks of male dominance (1988)" (66). Rather than seeing neutrality as an attempt to suspend identity and identification, a polarized binary logic is applied so that one is either supporting the oppressed or one is an oppressor.[69]

Coupled with this rejection of analytic neutrality, we find a criticism of the promotion of self-reliance and individual freedom in analysis: "Autonomy and dependency are raced as well as gendered in Western society. Altman (2010) suggests that the idealization of freedom and agency implicit in the American Dream requires a denial of natural dependency needs in service of maintaining a sense of total self-reliance. Inasmuch as self-reliance is bound up in the construction of a "good" white American self, anything that threatens that self-image must be disavowed" (66). Whereas there is much to critique about the libertarian ideology of free individualism, psychoanalysis is grounded on the unavoidable conflict between society and the individual.[70] Instead of taking one side or the other in this conflict, the analyst suspends judgment and allows the patient to freely explore this fundamental internal and external division. The desire of the analyst should not be to choose individual freedom over social obligation or society over the individual; this unresolvable dialectic cannot be erased or avoided.

Neutrality and Free Association

Just as we cannot escape the reality of the fundamental conflict between society and the individual, we should also affirm that psychoanalysis follows the modern solution to this problem by constructing social practices that seek to combine universality with the protection of the individual.[71] For instance, universal human rights aim to treat everyone the same by protecting their individual freedoms.[72] Likewise, psychoanalysis applies the same theories and practices to each case in order to clear a space for individual subjectivity to emerge. It is therefore hard to say that analytic neutrality and free association are inherently representing the interests of white, wealthy, heterosexual males since the aim of these practices is to avoid prejudice, identity, and identification by suspending judgment.[73] However, as Sue Grand argues in her chapter "Skin Memories," analytic neutrality is often seen now as an attempt to erase politics and culture from the clinic: "So I tried to have a colorless analysis, in a psychic world divorced from politics and culture. But in the United States, color blindness is wishful phantasm; this phantasm can actually negate the others' historical subjectivity (see K. Leary, 2002)" (103). The problem with this argument is that the analyst should not erase anything, and the patient should be free to voice any issue, including political and cultural ones.[74] The real problem often occurs when the analyst seeks to focus on particular concerns, which are often based on individual politics and biases.

Grand adds that in her own analysis, what she really wanted her analyst to do was to play the role of her lost grandmother so that she could overcome the trauma of separation through an imaginary identification: "From the beginning of my analysis, I needed a reparative bond of identification. I needed my analyst to be an intact Bubbie from Brooklyn. I was suffering from attachment trauma. I wanted a sense of sameness with my analyst, a sameness that was both familiar and safe" (103). Of course, many patients want to use analysis in order to heal old wounds through the creation of an ideal relationship with the analyst, but this desire only feeds the imaginary transference, and may not lead to the discovery of new, often-uncomfortable unconscious material.[75] Although it may sound that I am calling for the analyst to be simply cold, impersonal, and non-responsive, what should be stressed is that the analyst still has to show that he or she is listening to the patient, but this listening is done without judgment. There is thus a performance of a negative activity as one intentionally refuses to judge or satisfy the demand for love, knowledge, and recognition.[76]

Even if we do think that every aspect of a person's lived experience is shaped by race, gender, class, and sexual orientation, it does not matter since the patient is free to say whatever comes to mind, and the analyst is prohibited from controlling the direction of the free association. While the analyst might ask patients what they are thinking and feeling, the goal is to motivate free association and not to direct the discourse in a particular preconceived direction.[77] Of course, this limitation of the role of the analyst threatens the analyst's own narcissism, and this is one reason why therapists and psychoanalysts have such a hard time trusting the process.

Not only does the analyst have to give up on the pleasure of being admired for being the idealized one who knows and cares, but the temptation to validate the patient also has to be avoided.[78] This issue is brought up in Pratyusha Tummala-Narra's chapter "Intersectionality in the Immigrant Context": "Yet, it is critical for the therapist, when relevant, to validate that the client's distress stems from systemic injustice, and that distress derived from racism, xenophobia, sexism, transphobia, heterosexism, classism, and ableism is an appropriate response to injustice (Greene, 2012)" (136). It is unclear how the analyst can validate a patient's interpretation without falling into the position of the imaginary ego ideal or the social super-ego. After all, it is up to the patient to discover their own truth through the process of speaking without worrying about what the analyst thinks. Relying on the validation of the therapist functions to feed the transference and block self-discovery. Moreover, as Tummala-Narra points out, any response by the analyst could be shaped by the analyst's own socialization and rigid identity: "Interestingly, because of shared socialization experiences of compartmentalizing identity, the therapist and the client may selectively focus on only certain aspects of the other's identity" (135). The best way to avoid this dynamic is for the analyst to simply stop interpreting from a position of knowledge or identity, and this is done by basing all interpretations on the desire to promote the free association of the patient.[79] In fact, one reason why Lacan used to end his sessions early was that he wanted to push his patients to speak without censoring.[80] If you end a session when a patient is not free associating, you push them to dedicate their time in analysis to this particular practice instead of wasting their time speaking like they usually speak, which after all, has not helped them.[81]

However, the lack of belief in the analytic process comes out in the following passage: "For instance, a client's associations to the therapist's gender may be a core component of the transference, or a therapist's attention to the client's racial background may dominate the exploration of conflicts related to social class" (136). The issue here is why is the therapist paying attention to any particular issue when Freud called for the "free-floating attention" of the analyst. One answer to this question is that therapy is not analysis, but then we have to ask why is this chapter in a collection on psychoanalysis and intersectionality? Since the difference between therapy and psychoanalysis is never clearly stated, it is hard to know what actually guides the work of these practitioners.[82]

It has been one of the main arguments of this book that psychoanalysis is still guided by Freud's fundamental concepts, and these concepts continue to shape both the practice and the theory. This argument may be hard to accept in a time of moral relativism, but as we have seen, when people are not guided by a set of core theories, they can rationalize any practice.[83] From this perspective, the problem with incorporating intersectionality and identity politics into psychoanalysis is that it can result in a complete undermining of the fundamental theory guiding treatment. On the one hand, we do not need a commitment to identity politics to transform what is discussed in analysis because anything and everything should be voiced, yet on the other hand, intersectional theory can serve to prevent psychoanalytic treatment because it can demonize the practices of neutrality and free association.

The Limits of Identity Politics in Analysis

As highlighted in the collection, even when a therapist does focus on identity issues, this approach can itself be highly limiting: "The attention to singular aspects of identity impedes a deeper understanding of the full range of experiences among racial minority immigrants, including migration history; acculturation; immigration status; language; experiences of race, gender, sexuality, social class, and dis/ability; and differences across immigrant generations" (136). Instead of the therapist selecting a type or form of identity to emphasize, analytic neutrality allows for a more open mode of analysis.[84] However, Tummala-Narra undermines this approach by returning to the identity issues of the analyst: "Nevertheless, the therapeutic relationship offers a space in which multiple aspects of identity can be explored, but only insofar as therapists are willing to examine the multiplicity of their own identities and their experiences with privilege and marginalization" (136). The problem with this method is that it does not allow the analyst the ability to take on the position of being a blank screen or empty mirror.

What we often find rejected in post-Freudian forms of psychoanalysis and therapy is the notion that free association relies on the neutrality of the analyst, and this neutrality creates an unequal and asymmetrical relationship.[85] Rather than affirming the need for the analyst to suspend his or her own thought and subjectivity, we are told that the analyst also undergoes change while helping others to change: "Through this relationship, the therapist too is transformed as his/her/their own identity work is re-engaged" (137). At first, it appears that the analyst would have to change through working with others, but the analyst does not act as a "normal" person in analysis, and the analytic relationship is not a traditional relationship. Analytic neutrality requires taking on an artificial position, which is fortified by a clear understanding of analytic theory.[86] What we are seeing today is there is a lack of understanding concerning both the theory and the practice of psychoanalysis, and the result is that non-analytic concerns are interjected into the analytic process.

The central problem, then, with intersectionality and identity politics for psychoanalysis is that the focus on identity undermines the ability of free association and the free-floating attention of the analyst. Furthermore, as Freud discovered in his examination of the primary processes, consciousness is not controlled by the intentional ego, and so Lacan is correct to stress that the subject of psychoanalysis is barred and lacking.[87] In contrast to this lack of identity, Cleonie White focuses on the challenges posed by imposed identities in the immigrant experience: "My patient, Trevor, one might say, is "verbed"—that is, projected into performance of that position as in: "I speak, I think, I dream, I am immigrant." His position in culture is imposed as his defining identity. So, no matter how sturdy the immigrant's attempts to "integrate" into the new culture, he is met with repeated acts of rejection as his difference marks him the imperfect Other" (161). While we should not reject the difficulties of immigrant identity, it is vital to see that in relation to the unconscious and the primary processes, we are all immigrants lost in a foreign culture of strange representations.[88] However, the way to access this immigrant subjectivity is through free association and not a relationship of communication and identification.

In opposition to analytic neutrality, White calls for a relational approach to rethinking the immigrant experience: "Is it ever possible to articulate a different understanding of the construct "immigrant"— one that encompasses a conceptual framework less limited than that enveloped in imposed Otherness? Might we not regard this conceptual framework as, itself, embedded in hope and relational possibilities?" (161). Instead of turning to relationships as the key to re-imagining the role of immigrant subjectivity in therapy, psychoanalysis affirms that there is a fundamental non-relation between the self and the other.[89]

In fact, Lynne Layton's chapter brings to the foreground the inherent conflict between psychoanalysis and identity politics because political social movements need a strong identity, but analysis requires the temporary suspension of identity and identification.[90] Instead of affirming this fundamental aspect of analytic practice, Layton attacks Freudian theory for being the product of white, male, European privilege: "Indeed, I have become convinced over time that what primarily keeps alive the claim in our field that psychic reality can be understood without reference to social location is precisely the race and class privilege enjoyed by the dominant social groups to which our theory makers generally belong" (172). From this perspective, analytic neutrality is made possible by privilege and the repression of race and class concerns. However, with this rejection of analytic neutrality and free association, we see how identity politics can threaten the foundations of analysis itself.

It is vital to stress that I am not saying that race and class are not important topics for analysis; rather, my point is that any important issues will emerge in analysis if the analyst and the patent allow themselves to be open to every topic without censorship.[91] In fact, the focus on particular race and class issues by the analyst will only act to restrict the free exploration of the patient. In rejecting this foundation of analytic practice, Layton elaborates what other issues are essential to psychoanalytic treatment:

> I have taken relational understandings of the co-construction of analyses (e.g., Mitchell, 1988), of the patient's interpretation of the analyst's subjectivity (e.g., Aron, 1996; Hoffman, 1983), of the questioning of analytic authority (e.g., Hoffman, 1998), of the assumption that the therapist's

> unconscious bears significantly on the treatment, and of the belief in the inevitability of enactments and impasse (e.g., Levenson, 1972), and I have added to these tenets the suggestion that the unconscious and conscious micro-processes that mark all analytic sessions are inflected by culture and by the cultural inequalities within which subjectivity develops. (176)

Although it would be absurd to claim that culture does not affect what is said in analysis, the question is whether the analyst or therapist should direct the patient's discourse in any particular direction. I have argued that the analyst still needs to interpret, but these interventions are directed towards the sole purpose of promoting free association.[92] It is therefore misguided to see analysis as a co-construction equally concerned with the subjectivity of the analyst and the patient.

Notes

1. Belkin, Max, and Cleonie White, eds. *Intersectionality and relational psychoanalysis: New perspectives on race, gender, and sexuality*. Routledge, 2020.
2. Freud, Sigmund. *On the universal tendency to debasement in the sphere of love*. Read Books Ltd, 2014.
3. Samuels, Robert. "Pathos, Hysteria, and the Left." *Zizek and the Rhetorical Unconscious*. Palgrave Macmillan, Cham, 2020. 33–47.
4. Ryan, William. *Blaming the victim*. Vol. 226. Vintage, 1976.
5. Merrill, Roberto, and Daniel Weinstock. *Political Neutrality: A Re-evaluation*. Springer, 2014.
6. Israëls, Han, and Morton Schatzman. "The seduction theory." *History of Psychiatry* 4.13 (1993): 23–59.
7. Esterson, Allen. "Jeffrey Masson and Freud's seduction theory: a new fable based on old myths." *History of the Human Sciences* 11.1 (1998): 1–21.
8. Ferro, Antonino. *Seeds of illness, seeds of recovery: The genesis of suffering and the role of psychoanalysis*. Routledge, 2004.
9. Franklin, Girard. "The multiple meanings of neutrality." *Journal of the American Psychoanalytic Association* 38.1 (1990): 195–220.
10. Boothby, Richard. *Death and Desire (RLE: Lacan): Psychoanalytic Theory in Lacan's Return to Freud*. Routledge, 2014.

11. Smith, Joseph, H. "Ego psychology and the language of Lacan: transference and affect." *Psychoanalysis and contemporary thought* 14.1 (1991): 143–182.
12. Ian, Marcia. "Freud, Lacan, and imaginary secularity." *American Imago* 54.2 (1997): 123–147.
13. Caudill, D. ""Lacan's social psychoanalysis"." *The Subject of Lacan Eds K Malone, S Friedlander (State University of New York Press, Albany, NY) pp* (2000): 297–315.
14. Johnson, Barbara. *The feminist difference: Literature, psychoanalysis, race, and gender*. Harvard University Press, 1998.
15. Gerson, Samuel. "Neutrality, resistance, and self-disclosure in an intersubjective psychoanalysis." *Psychoanalytic Dialogues*6.5 (1996): 623–645.
16. Guralnik, Orna. "Sleeping dogs: Psychoanalysis and the socio-political." *Psychoanalytic Dialogues* 26.6 (2016): 655–663.
17. Flax, Jane. *Disputed subjects: Essays on psychoanalysis, politics and philosophy*. Routledge, 2012.
18. Rozmarin, Eyal. "Better identity politics." *Psychoanalytic Dialogues* 20.2 (2010): 181–190.
19. Grinberg, León, and Rebeca Grinberg. "The problem of identity and the psychoanalytical process." *International Review of Psycho-Analysis* 1 (1974): 499–507.
20. Akhtar, Salman. *Immigration and identity: Turmoil, treatment, and transformation*. Jason Aronson, 1999.
21. Jekels, Ludwig, and Edmund Bergler. "Transference and love." *The Psychoanalytic Quarterly* 18.3 (1949): 325–350.
22. Kohut, Heinz. *How does analysis cure?*. University of Chicago Press, 2009.
23. Schneider, Stanley. "Transference, counter-transference, projective identification and role responsiveness in the supervisory process." *The Clinical Supervisor* 10.2 (1993): 71–84.
24. Wilson, Mitchell. "The analyst's desire and the problem of narcissistic resistances." *Journal of the American Psychoanalytic Association* 51.1 (2003): 71–99.
25. Dervin, Daniel. "Where Freud was, there Lacan shall be: Lacan and the fate of transference." *American Imago* 54.4 (1997): 347–375.
26. Rodriguez, Leonardo, and Silvia Rodriguez. "On the transference." *Analysis* 1 (1989): 165–185.

27. Shill, Merton A. "Analytic neutrality, anonymity, abstinence, and elective self-disclosure." *Journal of the American Psychoanalytic Association* 52.1 (2004): 151–187.
28. Lynn, David J., and George E. Vaillant. "Anonymity, neutrality, and confidentiality in the actual methods of Sigmund Freud: A review of 43 cases, 1907–1939." *American Journal of Psychiatry* 155.2 (1998): 163–171.
29. Ivey, Gavin. "Transference-counter-transference constellations and enactments in the psychotherapy of destructive narcissism." *British journal of medical psychology* 72.1 (1999): 63–74.
30. Böhm, Tomas. "Inner and outer frame breaks— Counter-transference, enactments and whose life history?." *The Scandinavian psychoanalytic review* 27.1 (2004): 2–11.
31. Khoury, Maurice. "The desire of the analyst and counter-transference: from the mirroring analyst to the desiring analyst." *The Lacan Tradition.* Routledge, 2018. 189–206.
32. Australian Centre for Psychoanalysis. "The Position of the Analyst in the Transference." *Analysis* 4 (1993): 91–96.
33. Alvarez, Anne. "Problems in the use of the counter-transference: Getting it across." *Journal of Child Psychotherapy* 9.1 (1983): 7–23.
34. Frosh, Stephen. "Psychoanalysis, identity and citizenship." *Culture and citizenship* (2001): 62–73.
35. Samuels, Robert. "The Resistances to Psychoanalysis and Global Progress." *Freud for the Twenty-First Century*. Palgrave Pivot, Cham, 2019. 53–67.
36. Rabinovich, Diana. "What is a Lacanian clinic?." *The Cambridge Companion to Lacan* (2003): 208.
37. Mills, Jon. "Lacan on paranoiac knowledge." *Psychoanalytic Psychology* 20.1 (2003): 30.
38. Heath, Chip, and Dan Heath. "The curse of knowledge." *Harvard Business Review* 84.12 (2006): 20–23.
39. Moraitis, George. "The couch as a protective shield for the analyst." *Psychoanalytic Inquiry* 15.3 (1995): 406–412.
40. Hamburg, Paul. "Interpretation and empathy: reading Lacan with Kohut." *International journal of psycho-analysis* 72 (1991): 347–361.
41. Lacan, Jacques, Alan Sheridan, and Malcolm Bowie. "Aggressivity in psychoanalysis." *Ecrits*. Routledge, 2020. 9–32.

42. Owens, Carol, and Stephanie Swales. *Psychoanalysing ambivalence with Freud and Lacan: On and off the Couch*. Routledge, 2019.
43. Samuels, Robert. "Beyond Hillary Clinton: Obsessional Narcissism and the Failure of the Liberal Class." *Psychoanalyzing the Left and Right after Donald Trump*. Palgrave Macmillan, Cham, 2016. 31–59.
44. Samuels, Robert. "Transference and Narcissism." *Freud for the Twenty-First Century*. Palgrave Pivot, Cham, 2019. 43–51.
45. Natanson, Maurice. "Jean-Paul Sartre's Philosophy of Freedom." *Literature, Philosophy, and the Social Sciences*. Springer, Dordrecht, 1962. 62–75.
46. Fayek, Ahmed. "Narcissism and the death instinct." *International journal of psycho-analysis* 62 (1981): 309–322.
47. Fayek, Ahmed. "Narcissism and the death instinct." *International journal of psycho-analysis* 62 (1981): 309–322.
48. Sampson, Edward E. "Identity politics: Challenges to psychology's understanding." *American psychologist* 48.12 (1993): 1219.
49. Miller, Jacques-Alain, ed. *The Seminar of Jacques Lacan: Book 1: Freud's Papers on Technique 1953-1954*. CUP Archive, 1988.
50. Samuels, Robert. "Pathos, Hysteria, and the Left." *Zizek and the Rhetorical Unconscious*. Palgrave Macmillan, Cham, 2020. 33–47.
51. Freud, Sigmund. "'A child is being beaten'a contribution to the study of the origin of sexual perversions." *The Standard Edition of the Complete Psychological Works of Sigmund Freud, Volume XVII (1917-1919): An Infantile Neurosis and Other Works*. 1955. 175–204.
52. Cole, Alyson Manda. *The cult of true victimhood: From the war on welfare to the war on terror*. Stanford University Press, 2007.
53. Burke, Walter F. "Countertransference disclosure and the asymmetry/mutuality dilemma." *Psychoanalytic Dialogues* 2.2 (1992): 241–271.
54. Braunstein, Néstor. "Desire and Jouissance in the Teachings of Lacan." *The Cambridge Companion to Lacan* (2003): 102–115.
55. Basch, Michael F. "Affect and the analyst." *Psychoanalytic Inquiry* 3.4 (1983): 691–703.
56. Kohut, Heinz. "The psychoanalytic treatment of narcissistic personality disorders: Outline of a systematic approach." *The psychoanalytic study of the child* 23.1 (1968): 86–113.
57. Kernberg, Otto, F. "Further contributions to the treatment of narcissistic personalities." *International Journal of Psycho-Analysis* 55 (1974): 215–240.

58. Lacan, Jacques, Alan Sheridan, and Malcolm Bowie. "The Direction of the Treatment and the Principles of its Power 1." *Écrits*. Routledge, 2020. 250–310.
59. Freud, Sigmund. "Three essays on the theory of sexuality (1905)." *The standard edition of the complete psychological works of Sigmund Freud, volume VII (1901-1905): A case of hysteria, three essays on sexuality and other works*. 1953. 123–246.
60. Hekman, Susan. "Beyond identity: Feminism, identity and identity politics." *Feminist Theory* 1.3 (2000): 289–308.
61. Bondi, Liz. "Locating identity politics." *Place and the Politics of Identity*. Routledge, 2004. 89–106.
62. Samuels, Robert. "The Resistances to Psychoanalysis and Global Progress." *Freud for the Twenty-First Century*. Palgrave Pivot, Cham, 2019. 53–67.
63. Jarach, Lawrence. "Essentialism and the problem of identity politics." *The Anarchist Library* (2004).
64. Samuels, Robert. "Logos, global justice, and the reality principle." *Zizek and the rhetorical unconscious*. Palgrave Macmillan, Cham, 2020. 65–86.
65. Pagden, Anthony. *The Enlightenment: and why it still matters*. Oxford University Press, 2013.
66. Samuels, Robert. "Pathos, Hysteria, and the Left." *Zizek and the Rhetorical Unconscious*. Palgrave Macmillan, Cham, 2020. 33–47.
67. Dimen, Muriel. "The third step: Freud, the feminists, and postmodernism." *The American Journal of Psychoanalysis* 55.4 (1995): 303–319.
68. Chatterjee, Angana. "The Plausibility of a Feminist Philosopher's Take on Freudian Analysis." *Journal of Indian Council of Philosophical Research* 32.2 (2015): 227–237.
69. Samuels, Robert. "Pathos, Hysteria, and the Left." *Zizek and the Rhetorical Unconscious*. Palgrave Macmillan, Cham, 2020. 33–47.
70. Nock, Christopher John. "Equal freedom and unequal property: a critique of Nozick's libertarian case." *Canadian Journal of Political Science/Revue canadienne de science politique* 25.4 (1992): 677–695.
71. Bridge, Gary. "Rationality, ethics, and space: On situated universalism and the self-interested acknowledgement of 'difference'." *Environment and Planning D: Society and Space*18.4 (2000): 519–535.
72. Samuels, Robert. "Logos, global justice, and the reality principle." *Zizek and the rhetorical unconscious*. Palgrave Macmillan, Cham, 2020. 65–86.

73. Frosh, Stephen. "Facing political truths." *Psychotherapy and Politics International* 5.1 (2007): 29–36.
74. Samuels, Robert. "Global solidarity and global government: The universal subject of psychoanalysis and democracy." *Psychoanalyzing the left and right after Donald Trump*. Palgrave Macmillan, Cham, 2016. 77–101.
75. Colman, Warren. "Imagination and the imaginary." *Journal of Analytical Psychology* 51.1 (2006): 21–41.
76. Cooper, Seiso Paul. *Zen insight, psychoanalytic action: Two arrows meeting*. Routledge, 2018.
77. Lothane, Henry Zvi. "Free association as the foundation of the psychoanalytic method and psychoanalysis as a historical science." *Psychoanalytic Inquiry* 38.6 (2018): 416–434.
78. Moncayo, Raul. *Evolving Lacanian perspectives for clinical psychoanalysis: On narcissism, sexuation, and the phases of analysis in contemporary culture*. Routledge, 2018.
79. Stevens, Alexandre. "Lacanian interpretation." *Hurly-Burly: The International Lacanian Journal of Psychoanalysis* 1 (2009): 57–59.
80. Diatkine, Gilbert. "Lacan." *The International Journal of Psychoanalysis* 88.3 (2007): 643–660.
81. Skelton, Ross. "Lacan for the faint hearted." *British Journal of Psychotherapy* 10.3 (1994): 419–429.
82. Parker, Ian. *Lacanian psychoanalysis: Revolutions in subjectivity*. Routledge, 2010.
83. Harman, Gilbert. "What is moral relativism?." *Values and morals*. Springer, Dordrecht, 1978. 143–161.
84. Bass, Jeffrey D. *In exile from the self: Identity, politics, and psychoanalysis in Buenos Aires*. University of California, San Diego, 2000.
85. Bowker, Matthew H. "Analytical and Political Neutrality: Change, Privilege, and Responsibility." *Free Associations* 71 (2018): 1–17.
86. Hoffer, Axel. "Toward a definition of psychoanalytic neutrality." *Journal of the American Psychoanalytic Association* 33.4 (1985): 771–795.
87. Parker, Ian. "Jacques Lacan, barred psychologist." *Theory & Psychology* 13.1 (2003): 95–115.
88. Kandel, Eric. *The age of insight: The quest to understand the unconscious in art, mind, and brain, from Vienna 1900 to the present*. Random House, 2012.
89. Johnston, Adrian. "Analytic Action." *Irrepressible Truth*. Palgrave Macmillan, Cham, 2017. 151–168.

90. Samuels, Robert. "Trump and Sanders on the Couch: Neoliberal Populism on the Left and the Right." *Psychoanalyzing the left and right after Donald Trump*. Palgrave Macmillan, Cham, 2016. 61–76.
91. Adler, Elliot, and Janet L. Bachant. "Free Associatioan and Analytic Neutraltity: Basic Structure of the Psychoanalytic Situation." *Journal of the American Psychoanalytic Association* 44.4 (1996): 1021–1046.
92. Miller, Jacques-Alain. "A Reading of Some Details in Television in dialogue with the audience." *Newsletter of the Freudian Field* 4.1 (1990): 24–29.

8

Conclusion: Still (Mis)Understanding Psychoanalysis

The main argument of this book has been that psychoanalytic practice and theory is based primarily on five fundamental concepts, and when these principles are misunderstood, the specificity of this discourse is lost. As we have seen, one of the ways that Freud's original practice is undermined is through the refusal to accept the neutrality of the analyst, which enables the free association of the patient.[1] It turns out that many therapists and analysts today simply reject the very idea of suspending judgment and understanding in order to allow patients to say whatever comes into their minds. Perhaps it is the difficulty in giving up a position of power that prevents people from assuming the analytic position.[2]

The resistance to analytic neutrality has also been tied to the political claim that the concept of neutrality was derived from privileged white male Europeans, and so it must be a form of oppression and prejudice.[3] However, what Freud shows in his use of this notion is the idea that the reality principle requires a bias against bias, and so even if neutrality is the product of a particular culture and class, its power undermines all particular interests.[4] In fact, the concept of neutrality is a key aspect of seeing psychoanalysis as a science. Since the goal in modern science is to judge evidence from a neutral perspective, the need to suspend self-interest and

R. Samuels, *(Mis)Understanding Freud with Lacan, Zizek, and Neuroscience*, The Palgrave Lacan Series, https://doi.org/10.1007/978-3-031-13327-5_8

cultural values in the pursuit of truth and reality requires radical self-honesty, and we find this same driving force behind psychoanalytic practice and theory.[5]

In claiming that psychoanalysis is a science, I am countering the notion that this discipline has to turn to other fields in order to gain the respect that is granted to valorized sciences like neuroscience and evolutionary psychology. In fact, I have argued that these other respected discourses are often not actually sciences because they rely on a misguided understanding of human subjectivity.[6] Instead of seeing how humans make a break with biology and evolution through the open nature of their drives, many brain scientists seek to equate the human mind with the brains of other animals and computers.[7] Moreover, in the quest to determine the meaning of consciousness, they fail to see how the human mind is able to go beyond material reality when internal mental representations are confused with the perception of the external world. In repressing the psychoanalytic theory of the primary processes, these new disciplines seek to tie consciousness to inherited mental programs derived from natural selection.[8]

There is also the tendency in neuroscience and evolutionary psychology to conflate non-conscious mental process with the unconscious. As I have insisted throughout this book, the problem with this theory is that it excludes the essential notion of repression.[9] Since it is hard to understand how someone can lie to themselves, the splitting of the self between the truth and the lie is replaced by a simple acknowledgement of a lack of awareness. As I have shown, even an astute psychoanalyst like Lacan tends to confuse the unconscious with the primary processes, and one of the results of this conflation is that the ethical dimension of repression is lost.[10] Since we tend to repress thoughts and feelings that lead to shame and guilt, our protection of an idealized ego leads to a splitting of the self. As Freud first found in his work with hysterics, repression entails that not only do neurotic symptoms not make sense to the medical profession, but they also do not make sense to the subject.[11] In creating a break from anatomy and cognitive continuity, hysteria reveals the radical nature of human subjectivity.

Since neurotic symptoms manifest a gap between cause and effect, they provide a challenge to science and the medical disciplines. However, what we are seeing today is a repression of both hysteria and psychoanalysis itself as a result of the growing dominance of biological determinism coupled with the combination of capitalism and managed healthcare.[12] Since psychoanalysts and therapist often rely on insurance payments, they are forced to accept the standard model of diagnosis, which tends to eliminate psychoanalysis and privilege pharmaceutical solutions.[13] In turn, the pharmaceutical interests also rely on a biological model in order to base psychological disorders on chemical imbalances, and university researches rely on Big Pharma to support their research, while government agencies also push a medical model for mental health issues. The question of whether psychoanalysis is a science, then, has tremendous implications since a misguided notion of science drives the success of the brain sciences and the repression of psychoanalysis.

As Freud argued throughout his work, a key to science is the acceptance of the limitation of our knowledge.[14] This humility is required because we need to recognize that there is a fundamental difference between reality and our representations of reality. Moreover, since science is about discovering something new, it has to be open to encountering what it does not know.[15] The problem, then, with the new brain sciences is that they often claim to have total knowledge because they eliminate the difference between nature and culture. By claiming that our social and psychological reactions are derived from natural selection, the gap between reality and our representations is lost.[16] Meanwhile, the elimination of free will and social mediation results in an anti-social ideology where humans are conceived as being computerized animals who pursue pleasure and self-preservation at all costs. The paradox of this dominance of the pleasure principle is that the pursuit of total freedom and enjoyment ends up in total self-destruction.[17] As we see in the case of addictions, by giving into our drives and impulses, we end up harming ourselves and the people around us.[18]

Freud affirmed in his *Project for a Scientific Psychology* that the pleasure principle is determined by a law of inertia, which means that we are driven to use as little mental and physical energy as possible. Not only do we seek to outsource our physical labor to technology, but we are also seeking to outsource our minds to automation. The real meaning of the death drive, then, is that the pursuit of pleasure is equivalent to an escape from the self, the other, and reality.[19] Psychoanalysis is therefore needed more than ever because it is the only discourse that understands this self-destructive drive shaping human thought and behavior.

Unfortunately, as this book has documented, psychoanalysis is being repressed both inside and outside of psychoanalysis. Since its major concepts are easily misunderstood, it has been easy to see Freud's theory as being outdated; however, I hope I have shown that this vital discourse is still guided by a handful of essential concepts. Of course, many people will reject this argument because it idealizes Freud as the one who already always knows. Furthermore, if I pose myself as the only one who really understands Freud, then I only serve to heighten the idealizing transference. However, Freud's work also includes a safe-guard against identification and idealization. Since the goal of analysis is to allow for the free association of the patient, anything that prevents the free discovery of unconscious material must be considered to be a resistance to the truth itself. From this perspective, the discourse does not belong to Freud or any of his followers; rather, the theory provides a space for a practice that has no limits or inherent content. As a pure practice of radical self-honesty, psychoanalysis is an open discourse without identity or identification.

Notes

1. Poland, Warren S. "On the analyst's neutrality." *Journal of the American Psychoanalytic Association* 32.2 (1984): 283–299.
2. Lacan, Jacques, Alan Sheridan, and Malcolm Bowie. "The Direction of the Treatment and the Principles of its Power 1." *Écrits*. Routledge, 2020. 250–310.
3. Rose, Jeff, and Karen Paisley. "White privilege in experiential education: A critical reflection." *Leisure Sciences* 34.2 (2012): 136–154.
4. Samuels, Robert. "Science and the reality principle." *Freud for the twenty-first century*. Palgrave Pivot, Cham, 2019. 5–16.
5. Samuels, Robert. "Logos, global justice, and the reality principle." *Zizek and the rhetorical unconscious*. Palgrave Macmillan, Cham, 2020. 65–86.
6. Hughes, Austin L. "The folly of scientism." *The New Atlantis* (2012): 32–50.

7. Tallis, Raymond. *Aping mankind.* Routledge, 2016.
8. Misulia, Mark. "Aping Mankind: Neuromania, Darwinitis, and the Misrepresentation of Humanity." *First Things* 223 (2012): 65.
9. Anderson, Michael C. "Repression: A cognitive neuroscience approach." *Psychoanalysis and neuroscience.* Springer, Milano, 2006. 327–349.
10. Dor, Joël. *Introduction to the reading of Lacan: The unconscious structured like a language.* Other Press, LLC, 1998.
11. Freud, Sigmund. "Project for a scientific psychology (1950 [1895])." *The Standard Edition of the Complete Psychological Works of Sigmund Freud, Volume I (1886-1899): Pre-Psycho-Analytic Publications and Unpublished Drafts.* 1966. 281–391.
12. Horwitz, Allan V. *DSM: A History of Psychiatry's Bible.* JHU Press, 2021.
13. Samuels, Robert. "Drugging Discontent: Psychoanalysis, Drives, and the Governmental University Medical Pharmaceutical Complex (GUMP)." *Psychoanalyzing the Politics of the New Brain Sciences.* Palgrave Pivot, Cham, 2017. 115–136.
14. Freud, Sigmund. *Totem And Taboo: Some Points of Agreement between the Mental Lives of Savages and.* Routledge, 2013.
15. Moraitis, George. "Knowledge and ignorance in psychoanalysis." *The Annual of Psychoanalysis, V. 28* 28 (2013): 151.
16. Samuels, Robert. "The Backlash Politics of Evolutionary Psychology: Steven Pinker's Blank Slate." *Psychoanalyzing the Politics of the New Brain Sciences.* Palgrave Pivot, Cham, 2017. 35–58.
17. Rosenberg, Benno. "(Erotogenic) Masochism and the Pleasure Principle 1." *Reading French Psychoanalysis.* Routledge, 2014. 516–527.
18. Mills, Jon. "Reflections on the death drive." *Psychoanalytic Psychology* 23.2 (2006): 373.
19. Fromm, Erich. *Escape from freedom.* Macmillan, 1994.

Index

R. Samuels, *(Mis)Understanding Freud with Lacan, Zizek, and Neuroscience*, The Palgrave Lacan Series, https://doi.org/10.1007/978-3-031-13327-5

The manufacturer's authorised representative in the EU is Springer Nature Customer Service Centre GmbH, Europaplatz 3, 69115 Heidelberg, Germany. If you have any concerns regarding our products, please contact ProductSafety@springernature.com

Printed and bound by CPI Group (UK) Ltd, Croydon, CR0 4YY
30/09/2026
02225243-0001